The Last Laker

Finding a Wreck Lost in the Great Lakes' Deadliest Storm

by Frederick Stonehouse

Lake Superior
Port Cities Inc.

©2015 Frederick Stonehouse

All rights reserved. No part of this publication may be reproduced or transmitted in any form or by any means, electronic or mechanical, including photocopying, recording or any information storage and retrieval system, without permission in writing from the publisher.

First Edition: June 2015

Lake Superior Port Cities Inc.
P.O. Box 16417
Duluth, Minnesota 55816-0417 USA
888-BIG LAKE (888-244-5253)

5 4 3 2 1

Library of Congress Cataloging-in-Publication Data

Stonehouse, Frederick, 1948-
    The last laker : finding a wreck lost in the great lakes' deadliest storm / by Frederick Stonehouse – First edition.
        pages cm
    Includes bibliographical references and index.
    ISBN 978-1-938229-23-7
    1. Storms – Great Lakes (North America) – History – 20th century.
    2. Great Lakes (North America) – History – 20th century.
    3. Shipwrecks – Great Lakes (North America) – History – 20th century. I. Title.
    F551.L375 2015
    910.977 – dc23   2015007387

Editors: Paul L. Hayden, Konnie LeMay, Ann Possis
Design: Tanya Bäck, cover; Amy Larsen, interior
Photos: All internal images Author's Collection, unless noted
Printer: Friesens, printed in Canada

Dedication

To the "Storm Warriors" of Eagle Harbor and Portage
Life-Saving stations, men with extraordinary courage.
"Regulations say we have to go out,
they say nothing about coming back."

And to wreck hunters three:
Jerry Eliason, Ken Merryman and Kraig Smith.
Searching, ever searching for the ones still missing.

And finally to the
Lost Crew of the *Henry B. Smith*

James Owen	Chris Leofen
Charles Cattanach	James McGee
George Carey	Matt Maralick
Peter Costandakis	Charles J. Nilsen
John Cousins	Andrew Olsen
Martin Freeman	John H. Olsen
John Gallagher	Lawrence Perry
H.H. Haskin	Charles E. Rayburn
Carl Hoppel	Edward Shipley
Rufus Judson	John Shirl
Otto Julius	John Tait
Roy Kelly	Joseph Zink

Plus two whose names are unknown

Advance Praise for *The Last Laker*

Frederick Stonehouse is the dean of Great Lakes shipwreck historians and a prolific author. His books are instant classics, and reflect not only his skill as a writer, but also his careful research, eye for detail and his years of experience dealing with the lakes and its ships. *The Last Laker* is a tremendous book, telling the story of the ship and its people, and of the long search to resolve the mystery of where the *Smith* was and what happened to it. While Stonehouse is careful to not try and definitively say exactly what did happen – for indeed, dead men often tell no tales, and the wreck has not and may not ever yield all of its secrets – this is a tour de force of thoughtful possibilities and probabilities, and a tribute to the men of the *Smith* as well as the dedicated team who at last found the wreck.

– **James P. Delgado, PhD**
Director of Maritime Heritage,
NOAA's Office of National Marine Sanctuaries

Fred Stonehouse is not one to be content in merely recounting the story of the loss of the *Henry B. Smith* and the recent discovery of her final resting place. Of course, Fred covers both subjects in spades, but he also takes us on an enthralling and far-reaching journey of discovery in which he analyzes the evolution in the design of Great Lakes freighters and how those design decisions may have impacted the loss of the vessel, while using the results of the most recent computer weather models in breaking down exactly what made the Storm of 1913 the true storm of the century, and how its deadly blow wreaked havoc throughout the length and breadth of the lakes. Sure, it's a page-turner, as you would expect from a Stonehouse book, but it just may also be the definitive book on the great blow of 1913. In the words of a couple of Windy City newspaper men - TWO THUMBS UP!

– **Terry Pepper**
Lighthouse Historian and Executive Director of the
Great Lakes Lighthouse Keepers Association

Using new information, Fred Stonehouse sets the stage for the lethal 1913 weather bomb, establishes the reach of the storm with broader strokes, then zeros in on the ill-fated *Henry B. Smith* as her captain and crew sail out of Marquette and into Lake Superior legend. Stonehouse knows how to tell a compelling story, and he does so without ever losing sight of the facts. Impeccably researched and compellingly told, this is the best book on the 1913 storm I've read.

– **Roger LeLievre**
Publisher *Know Your Ships* & editor *Great Laker Magazine*

Table of Contents

	Introduction vi
Chapter 1	The Long Search 1
Chapter 2	Life and Times of the *Henry B. Smith* 8
Chapter 3	When the Lakes Ran Wild 34
Chapter 4	Huron Moaned. 52
Chapter 5	Superior Screamed 74
Chapter 6	Fate Will Choose. 88
Chapter 7	Picking Up the Pieces 124
Chapter 8	What Happened 138
Chapter 9	Mystery Solved 184
	Endnotes 197
	Bibliography. 204
	Index. 209
	About the Author 215

Introduction

I originally had no intention of writing a Storm of 1913 book. Of course, I was fascinated, like so many intrigued by maritime history, by the details of the storm and its destruction of vessels with all hands (12) and lives (256) on the Great Lakes. Even though the centennial was coming up, I saw no compelling reason to rehash essentially old material. The storm was well documented with several fine books covering the entire event and a large number of various publications closely examining individual wrecks. The Storm of 1913 was a tale well told. Then several things happened.

On May 24, 2013, the last of the storm-lost lakers, the 525-foot *Henry B. Smith,* was discovered by a team of dedicated shipwreck hunters. (Rumor already had it that another of the seven bulk lake freighters lost, *James Carruthers,* had been found, though the searchers remain mum on that one.) Of all the 1913 losses, the *Smith* was my favorite and by my consideration, the last of the undiscovered lakers gone missing in that storm. She left the fewest clues about her loss and her complete disappearance is, to my view, the most inexplicable. I also consider her the most sought-after wreck. At various times a number of private search efforts failed to find her as did the U.S. Navy on two occasions. From this viewpoint she could be called the "ghost ship" of the storm; she is the "gold" of all the ships lost.

How this crew found the *Smith* helped me see that the Storm of 1913 could be a real mystery book. When I thought about the wreck's location and considered it in relation to that of the steamer *L.C. Waldo* and the heroic effort of the U.S. Life-Saving Service to save the latter's crew, I realized that there was a tantalizing "what might have been" scenario, too. This is a different way of tying two compelling stories together.

I also noticed that the Storm of 1913 books that were published during the centennial either only mentioned the *Smith* discovery in passing or, depending on the printing date, not at all. Their omission was one I could correct.

The more I examined the *Smith* wreck and the video of her remains, the more I realized the eerie similarities to the wreck of the *Cyprus,* lost in 1907. I saw a linkage that should be further explored and explained. Oddly enough, after locating the *Smith,* the team moved to the eastern part of Lake Superior to check out other process-identified targets. One of them turned out to be the *Cyprus.* Although she was found in 2007, the latitude/longitude numbers were never released, so in effect she was discovered for a second "first time" by the *Smith* team. A fascinating coincidence!

Lastly, the National Oceanic and Atmospheric Administration (NOAA), as part of the centennial, pushed all the available weather data for the 1913 storm through a simulation program, producing a far more complete understanding of wind and wave conditions as the weather monster played out. This, too, was not included in any of the 1913 books. Incorporating this information into the story has provided a different and important perspective.

All this considered, I decided it was worthwhile to write this book, and if you open your mind to it, you can also discover the "who-dun-it."

Frederick Stonehouse
May 2015

CHAPTER 1

The Long Search

The last century saw numerous efforts to solve the mystery of the loss and location of the *Henry B. Smith*. Where is she? What really happened to her? Although some searches were more serious than others, all would ultimately fail. Untold hours of scouring the bottom of the lake came up empty. Backtracking wreckage found ashore using known wind speeds and direction, and computing the data with drift analysis software programs, also were unsuccessful. The last of the big lakers in the 1913 storm continued to evade detection, hiding deep in Lake Superior's icy depths. The big steamer was down there somewhere … waiting!

Where is the massive *Henry B. Smith?*

The *Smith* was a tantalizing enigma of the lakes begging to be solved. Many folks took the challenge and tried their best. The first serious efforts involved using "scanning sonar," the scanning portion housed in a dome projecting from the bottom of the search vessel. Pulses from the scanner bounced off objects on the

The U.S. Navy P-3 Orion is a highly capable search aircraft.

MARQUETTE MARITIME MUSEUM COLLECTION

bottom displaying on a large cathode ray tube (round TV screen) in the boat, much as radar targets are shown. While the technology worked to a point, it was essentially "generation one" and soon became outdated.

The new and improved technology involved towing a side-scanning sonar behind a boat. The "towfish" is usually a finned conical or tubular device towed near (slightly above) the seabed while emitting fan-shaped pulses toward the sea floor across a wide angle perpendicular to the path of the sensor through the water. The returns from the fan-shaped beam are in turn transmitted back to a recording device in the boat. Objects detected are represented by their shadow "painted" on the recorder. Often called "mowing the grass," it is a mind-numbing job, and usually fruitless. Over time side-scanning technology improved dramatically in capability, but still was unable to find the *Smith*.

In 1987, at the behest of a local shipwreck group largely led by diver and researcher Randy Beebe, the U.S. Navy even used a P-3 Orion submarine-hunting aircraft in a search effort. The Navy treated the effort as a valuable training opportunity. It was long rumored in the Great Lakes diving community that the Navy routinely used steel shipwrecks in the Great Lakes as practice targets, including those missing. The Navy didn't know whether a wreck was a "ghost" ship or not. They just knew it as a target.

For a time, many Great Lakes divers were convinced that the P-3 squadrons had classified lists of target locations throughout the lakes. Rather than make the long and time consuming flights to the East or West coasts for training, they just used the local steel wrecks. Questioned by researchers, the Navy denied all knowledge of the special target lists, but then again many divers thought, "Why would they admit it?" A U.S. Navy Lockheed P-3 Orion aircraft quickly found the wreck of the *Edmund Fitzgerald* on November 14, 1975, four days after her tragic loss.

From 1970 to 1990, Glenview Naval Air Station in Glenview, Illinois, was home to two Naval Air Reserve squadrons (Patrol Squadrons 60 and 90). Initially equipped with P-2 Neptunes, they later transitioned to P-3A and P-3B Orions. The squadrons routinely deployed to the Atlantic, Mediterranean and Caribbean for anti-submarine operations against Soviet submarines and surface craft. The base closed as the result of a 1993 base realignment and closure decision.

The P-3 Orion is a four-engine turboprop anti-submarine and maritime surveillance aircraft developed by Lockheed for the U.S. Navy and introduced in the 1960s. The P-3 Orion is in use by numerous navies and air forces around the world.

The P-3 airframe is based on the old Lockheed Electra. Most distinctive is the tail stinger or "MAD Boom," used for the magnetic detection of submarines.[1] Reputedly their highly sophisticated magnetic anomaly detection (MAD) equipment is capable of locating Russian submarines (equipped with magnetic-shielded hull coatings) lurking deep under the northern ice pack. Regardless, the P-3 couldn't find a 525-foot steel ore carrier filled with rich iron ore in Lake Superior. Go figure.

The Navy still uses the P-3 today and numerous design advancements, most notably to its electronics packages, have been added. It is also among a handful

Discussing the search plan – Dan Fountain, Randy Beebe and naval aircrew.

MARQUETTE MARITIME MUSEUM COLLECTION

of aircraft, including the Boeing B-52 Stratofortress and Boeing KC-135 Stratotanker, that have passed the 50-year mark and continue in frontline service. She will eventually be replaced by the Boeing P-8A Poseidon.[2]

A second Navy effort was made in 1999 by the USS *Defender*. Known as an MCM (Mine Counter-Mine) vessel, she was charged and equipped to locate and neutralize enemy sea-based mines, an ideal candidate to find the long-lost steamer. The 224-foot ships are fiberglass sheathed, wooden-hull construction, the non-metallic hulls helping to defeat magnetic mines. *Defender* was on the Great Lakes as part of a Navy recruiting tour and used the *Smith* search as an opportunity to flex her search capability.[3] Using a vessel like the *Defender* for recruiting duty can be incredibly boring for the crew. While some of the crew is at least doing what it would normally do in terms of the deck crew handling lines, engineering running the various machinery and wheelhouse folks "driving the boat," the crew charged with operating the sophisticated search technology (the heart and soul of the ship in terms of mission) is literally sitting on its hands. Looking for the *Smith* gave the techies a chance to exercise their mission skills. Regardless of their best efforts, they also failed to find the wreck. Go figure again.

The Mine Counter-Mine (MCM) vessel USS *Defender*.

Searchers plotted wreckage locations and known weather conditions using Coast Guard Search and Rescue drift analysis techniques right out of the approved training manuals to no avail. One prominent university even tried a more sophisticated approach without success. The data was just too sparse to point to the *Smith*.

One group of intrepid *Smith* hunters even resorted to a séance, literally sitting around a table at midnight, holding hands with a medium, calling up the spirits of the crew. Although, supposedly, contact was made with Captain Owen, the effort didn't lead to finding the lost *Smith*.

In the meantime, through the decades there were various reports of fishermen fouling their nets or lines on strange shipwreck-like objects on the lake bottom. Other shipwreck-shaped targets were occasionally "painted" by chart-recording fish finders. Historians and divers spent many pleasant hours poring over Lake Superior charts speculating as to where the elusive *Smith* was hidden, time usually enhanced by inspiring glasses of spirits (of the liquid kind).

Some folks believe that she is one of Lake Superior's fleet of ghost ships, vessels that sailed off into a crack in the lake never to be seen again except on those dark storm-striven nights when their spectral images emerged again for brief moments before fading back to seas of lost ships and crews. I have a friend who swears that she has seen the *Smith*, passing downbound just off the harbor in the dead of night with all lights ablaze. She watched silently as the big steamer bucked into the storm, waves smashing off the bow sending quick flashes of white into the black air. And then it was gone, just winking into nothing. To this day, she is adamant that it was the *Smith*, and just to add a chill, it was on the anniversary of the *Smith*'s departure. Such is the life of a ghost ship.

But when all was said and done, the question remained. Where was the *Smith*?

All things in their due course. It was worldwide news when the *Henry B. Smith* was finally found on May 24, 2013. Media outlets everywhere trumpeted the discovery. A century after her loss, one of the last of the lost sisters of the storm finally "made port."

And it all came about through the work of a small, dedicated group of shipwreck hunters. The team literally committed decades of time to the slow and methodical effort to solve the mysteries of many Great Lakes ships that, as the old sailors said, "sailed through a crack in the lake."

However, it wasn't easy to find the *Smith*, and to get there we need to unravel all of the clues in this mystery that lay before us. As with any good mystery, we need to incorporate Sherlock, obtaining base information to build our case, the whys and wherefores of the events surrounding the disappearance and the probable motive and conclusions that can be drawn. From that we'll find the answers and then join the shipwreck hunters in their successful game.

Chapter 2

Life and Times of the *Henry B. Smith*

Moving Ore

The *Henry B. Smith* was born into the fast-paced world of Great Lakes shipping innovation. Progress was exploding as the Lake Superior iron mines became more and more critical to the building of America. Industry demanded steel, and steel drove the fleets of hundreds of bulk freighters filled with iron ore bound for the belching furnaces of lower lakes mills. The *Smith* was part of that immense system.

It all started in 1844 with the discovery of the vast and rich Marquette Iron Range in Michigan's rugged Upper Peninsula. Not long after that, the port of Marquette was established to ship the ore from the county's rapidly expanding mines. Later ore from other Upper Peninsula iron ranges joined the inexorable flood to the cauldrons of boiling metal. The ore was called "natural" or "direct shipping ore," reflecting that it was greater than 60 percent iron, pure enough to be fed directly into the furnaces.

This led to one unnamed historian commenting that the U.P. made its living for 150 years selling rocks and wood, rock meaning the iron and copper, and the wood and lumber from the boundless forests. Although copper is largely no longer sold, other than the just-opened nickel-copper Eagle Mine, iron is still shipped, but in pelletized form rather than directly shipping the rock of days long gone. Wood continues to be harvested.

After the initial discovery, the ore wasn't shipped downlake in any great amount until two tons arrived

The brigantine *Columbia* carried the first cargo of Marquette Range ore through the Soo Locks in 1855.

in Cleveland in 1852 ... in wood barrels! The handling required was absurd. After being blasted loose from the rock by explosives, it was clawed out from the mine with pick and shovel, dumped into wheelbarrows, pushed to a wagon and loaded by hand shovels into barrels. A horse team slowly and carefully dragged the wagon over horrible two-rutted trails 15 miles or so to the Marquette dock, where the barrels were laboriously hoisted aboard a schooner. Reaching the rapids of the St. Marys River, they were painstakingly unloaded from the schooner, reloaded on wagons and portaged around the rapids then reloaded on a waiting down-rapids vessel. If necessary, the original schooner was dragged on rollers, pulled by ox teams, around the rapids, too. The entire process around the rapids could take a month. At Cleveland the barrels were again lifted out of the schooner and reloaded on wagons for delivery to the iron furnace.

With the completion of the Soo Canal in 1855 the ore remained on the schooner for a quick passage, but there still was a large amount of cargo handling required.

The Sault Ste. Marie Locks circa 1860.
SUPERIOR VIEW STUDIO

All of which greatly added to the cost of transportation and viability of the ore in the marketplace.

There was a vast quantity of high-grade iron ore in the Marquette Range and others yet to be exploited, but how to bring it efficiently to market was the overwhelming test.

Regardless of the challenge, the high quality of the ore made it all worthwhile. Simply said, it was the premier quality iron ore in the country and there was an immense supply in the Marquette Iron Range. As a result, the annual production of the Lake Superior mines ballooned from a mere 1,449 tons in 1855 to nearly 2 million tons in 1880. As other Lake Superior ranges came into production, tonnage soared, reaching 7.3 million in 1889 and just under 80 million in 1913.

Soon new ship designs such as the steamer *R.J. Hackett,* built in Cleveland in 1869, revolutionized the movement of ore from dock to mill. Large hatches amidships made loading far more efficient, while powerful steam engines kept the ship moving through

weather fair or foul. Ships could now keep to a schedule and the mills could depend on a steady supply of ore.

When loading the ore on ships with wheelbarrows and "Norwegian steam"[1] could no longer keep up the pace, a wily inventor developed the pocket dock; railroad hopper cars dump the ore into steel "pockets" built into the dock. When a ship pulls alongside, long chutes drop from the pockets and shoot the ore into the cargo holds rapidly and efficiently. The first such docks were built in Marquette in 1862. As improvements were made

(Top) Marquette ore dock circa 1870. Note the schooners loading ore and the sidewheelers alongside the freight dock.
(Bottom) Rail hopper cars delivered the ore to the top of the dock then dropped it into "pockets."

A schooner-barge beside a lower harbor ore dock. Note the pocket chutes in place.

over time, such docks became commonplace in the Lake Superior iron ports.

Growth was phenomenal. In 1913 Marquette loaded 536 boats between the brand new Lake Superior and Ishpeming Railroad dock (LS&I) at Presque Isle and the Duluth, South Shore and Atlantic dock downtown. The LS&I dock was built in 1912 and is still in operation at this writing. 1913 was a bit of a down year for ore from the city. The year before, it loaded 60 more boats with more than 3.2 million tons of ore.

But getting the ore out of the ships' holds at the steel mill in the early days was still done with picks, shovels, wheelbarrows and more Norwegian steam. It was too slow and too inefficient. The mills demanded a better method.

Engineer Alexander E. Brown developed the first mechanical unloader in Cleveland in the 1870s. It was a simple steam-powered overhead cable system that dropped a bucket into the hold where it was hand-loaded, then lifted out and dumped dockside. Although it was a vast improvement decreasing unloading costs by roughly a factor of three, it still was far from efficient. Later a grab bucket was added, further increasing speed of unloading, but men still were needed to hand shovel in the last of the cargo. The amount of ore arriving at the docks outpaced the ability to unload it, not only at Cleveland but Ashtabula, Lorain and Fairport, too. Ships were wasting time and money waiting their turn to unload.

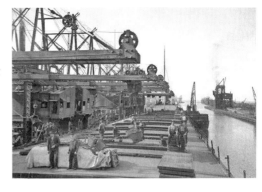

An early "whirley" unloader. Note the stacked wood hatch covers.

Some docks built track-mounted steam derricks called "whirleys." Equipped with grab buckets, they moved along the tracks to position themselves over the hatches to clam the ore out. But they could only dump it close to the ship, requiring the cargo to be handled again before finally reaching the furnaces.

Other docks went to a system called a "Champion hoist." It consisted of a wood A-frame that tilted over a ship, dropping a bucket into the hold. When loaded the bucket was elevated, the frame was pulled vertical and then dumped onto to an elevated platform. But the bucket was still hand-loaded.

Alexander Brown, the fellow who invented the first mechanical unloader, had a better idea. Called a "Brown Fast Plant," it was an electrically powered overhead rail system that carried an operator with drop bucket. The operator ran the bucket over the hold, clammed up a scoop of ore, then moved back to a rail car, where he jettisoned the ore or dropped it onto the dock for storage.

Capacity was a remarkable 3,600 tons a day. Fast Plants were used in many ports, including Cleveland, Lorain, Toledo and Ashtabula.[2]

But still the ore boats flooded into the steel ports, clamoring to unload and turn north again for more ore. The beast of American industry was insatiable.

The Hoover and Mason Company of Chicago leaped ahead of the others with a traveling bridge crane. It used a heavy automatic grab bucket with a bite of 18 cubic feet. A scraping motion completed the closure.[3]

The ultimate in unloading machinery was the "Hulett," invented by George H. Hulett. When it went into service in Cleveland in 1899, it revolutionized the unloading process. Its 10-ton bucket could scoop out 275 tons of ore an hour. Like the Hoover and Mason, it was a steel-bridge unit, but uniquely the operator rode the bucket into the cargo hold in a small cab. Later developments included a 17-ton bucket and an increased capacity of 1,000 tons an hour.[4]

The very design of ships changed to facilitate loading and unloading of ore. More and bigger hatches were added to the spar or weather deck to allow quick access to the holds for the pocket dock chutes and unloading clamshells. Eventually hatches were standardized at 12-foot centers. While the increased number and size of hatches added a degree of efficiency, they also compromised safety, but more on that later.

It must be remembered that there is a critical difference between ocean bulk carriers and lakers in terms of operational tempo. Lakers are (or should be) in constant motion. Trips are often only a week or less in duration, a quick port turnaround to load or unload and on again to repeat the cycle. This means vessel design must support the required tempo. By contrast, ocean bulkers can be steaming a month or more between ports and spend a comparatively long duration dockside. While a laker loads at a state-of-the-art ore dock and unloads with several Huletts working simultaneously, the ocean bulker may load at a remote dock with human labor, and the unload can be much the same.[5] Given the less

A set of Hulett electric unloaders in Conneaut, Ohio.

stress on time, hatches can be fewer and less efficient for loading or unloading than a laker would require. For example, 24-foot or more centers versus 12-foot centers.

The speed in loading ore via the new pocket docks and unloading with the various mechanical devices put added pressure on the ships. Less and less time was being spent in port at either end of the trip, with turnarounds measured in mere hours. The expensive part was now the trip itself. Each additional trip a ship could make per season increased the profits of the company. And larger ships meant increased efficiency and economy of scale, so pressure shifted to the maritime architects to design, and shipyards that could build, bigger and bigger bulk freighters.

The Ships

While the 1869 wooden-built *R.J. Hackett* is usually considered the prototypical Great Lakes bulk freighter with pilothouse forward, engines aft and cargo holds and hatches midships, she didn't keep her leadership position long.

The first iron freighter, *Onoko,* slid down the launch ways in 1882, setting a new standard of construction and operation. Her 2,136 tons gave her the greatest capacity of any vessel on the lakes, though many mariners thought

The steamer *Onoko* was the first iron lake freighter.

her ugly beyond description. I guess the critics missed the beauty of her utility.

Since most of the Great Lakes shipyards were located in steel manufacturing areas such as Cleveland, Lorain and Toledo, builders and designers were well aware of the potential that the new metal offered for shipbuilding and had easy access to the product direct from the mills. Steel supply would not normally be a problem. In 1888, for example, the Globe Iron Works in Cleveland was capable of building six big steel steamers a year.

The first steel freighter, the 1,741-ton *Spokane,* was launched only two years prior. She proved well found and long lived, finally scrapping out in 1935. Not to be outdone, later the same year the Buffalo Union Dry Dock Company pushed the 2,780-ton *Susquehanna* off the ways. The race was on as more and more steel steamers poured from the yards.

Engines also dramatically increased in power, too. Prior to 1880, the typical engine was a low-pressure single cylinder affair. Around this time new dual (or compound) cylinder engines appeared, in which steam was vented from the first cylinder to the second, increasing efficiency and power. In 1887, the same concept was expanded to a third cylinder with excellent results. Called triple expansion engines, they, too, vastly improved efficiency and power. The principle eventually grew to quadruple expansion engines.

As the ships grew bigger, the federal government responded by increasing the size of locks, canals and channels. The critical bottleneck at the Soo was eliminated when Congress authorized a fourth lock in 1912. The growling maw of the American Industrial Revolution called for more iron ore, and bigger waterways were critical for delivery.

Although the ore ships had only recently made the huge leaps from wooden ships to iron to steel, a feeling of invulnerability pervaded the industry. With ships as powerful as the steel monsters flowing out of the yards, the captains could certainly bull their way through any gale. Technology would always prevail over nature. As a result of the 1913 storm, this attitude would change!

The big steel lakers made an average of 30 round trips a year between the Lake Superior ore docks and lower lakes mills, often returning with coal, if possible, to avoid an unprofitable empty haul (aka running "light"). Smaller freighters owned by independent operators and concerns only averaged 20 round trips, but still earned a profit, contributing to the river of iron downbound to the fiery furnaces.

When the 540-foot, 6,585-ton *Augustus B. Wolvin* came down the ways at the Lorain yard of American Ship Building in 1904, she set the standard for the next six decades. Soon others of the new 600-foot class were commonplace. It was said a single one of these new behemoths could carry a cargo equal to the combined capacity of all of the vessels on Lake Superior at the beginning of the Civil War. In 1895, the average iron ore cargo was 1,800 tons. By 1912 it had jumped to 7,740 tons, all the result of the new bigger freighters. Marine men joked that the shipyards built them by the mile and just cut them off to whatever length the owner desired.[6]

The American Ship Building Company led the way to increased efficiency in shipbuilding, growing rapidly as demand for ships increased. Starting in Cleveland as the Cleveland Ship Building Company in 1888, it changed its name to American Ship Building a dozen years later. Eventually it acquired the Superior Ship

Building (Superior, Wisconsin), Toledo Ship Building (Toledo, Ohio), West Bay Ship Building (Bay City, Michigan), Globe Iron Works (Cleveland), Ship Owners Dry Dock Company (Cleveland), Buffalo Dry Dock (Buffalo), Chicago Ship Building (Chicago) and Detroit Ship Building (Wyandotte, Michigan). To many folks American Ship was shipbuilding on the Great Lakes.

The new bulk freighters came out at a prodigious rate. Between 1896 and 1910, 300 rumbled down the launchways, more than half during the 1905-10 period. Ship size grew also, from 500-footers in the start of the building frenzy to just over 600 feet in 1910.[7] They were building the ships so fast that sometimes the yards ran out of steel! And remember, in many instances the shipyard was next to the steel mill.

Marquette ore docks grew by leaps and bounds driven by the insatiable demand for iron.

The ships, of course, were all riveted rather than welded together. The new electric welding technology wouldn't see broad use in shipbuilding until the run-up to World War II. Even though it was more efficient, it required a massive new investment, not only in equipment but also training shipyard workers. It was easier to do it the old way even if the old riveted ships paid a significant penalty. For example, a 9,500-gross-ton riveted ship carried 600,000 to 700,000 rivets,

The American Ship Building yard in Lorain, Ohio.

which made her 500 tons heavier than a welded one of comparable size. The additional weight also came from the necessary overlap of hull plates for the rivets to join. The 500 tons of extra weight she was lugging around was 500 tons of less cargo, a significant loss in efficiency. In terms of tensile strength, welded plates were 90-95 percent of the original plate, while riveted ones were only 65-70 percent.[8]

There was also was a change in deck hatches. On the earlier bulk freighters they were set on 24-foot centers, but to better accommodate the new pocket dock loading chutes, the standard was shifted to 12 feet. The old 24 configuration meant that the ships had to shift back and forth frequently while alongside the loading dock to best position the chutes. The new 12s greatly lessened shifting, speeding up the loading process. And, of course, time is money.

The 12-foot centers also necessitated a change in construction. Instead of upright stanchions and traverse framing or web, arching girders were used under the weather deck.[9] This further increased unloading speed.

Since any hole in a ship can potentially admit water, adding more hatches only increased the possibility of flooding into the cargo hold, especially with boarding seas on the weather deck. Whether the designers and builders spent enough effort solving this potential problem is debatable.

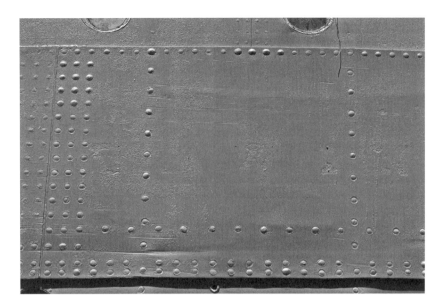

The rivet pattern on the *John B. Ford* (old *Edwin F. Holmes*) clearly shows the plate overlap common during the period.

STEVE HAVERTY/GREAT LAKES STEAMSHIP SOCIETY

To make the new big freighters pay they had to make quick trips and carry as much cargo as possible. Fast to load at the docks, efficient on the water and fast to unload at the mills. A captain waiting patiently in port for good weather worked against the critical need for speed. The freighters were built to punch through the worst that the lakes could offer and that's what they were expected to do. As events proved, however, expectations are not always correct.

The *Henry B. Smith*

Built in 1906 as hull No. 343 at the Lorain, Ohio, yard of American Ship Building Company, 6,631-ton *Henry B. Smith* was under the management of brothers William A. and Henry A. Hawgood of Cleveland. The firm, usually just known as "Hawgoods," managed a number of freighters and was considered a responsible and competent concern. William served as an alternate member of the influential executive committee of the Lake Carriers' Association in 1913.

The construction of the *Smith* was typical of her class. Length on the deck was 525 feet, beam 55 feet and depth 31 feet.[10] She was powered by a coal-burning, hand-fired

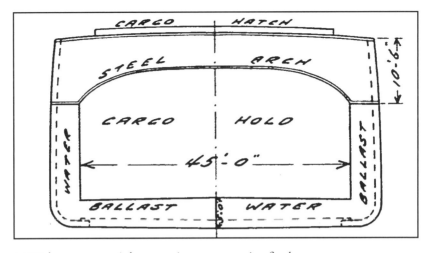

1,700-horsepower triple expansion steam engine fired by two Scotch boilers. The steam moved progressively through high, intermediate and low pressure cylinders, thus was called a triple expansion engine. The engine was identical to those of the Hawgood laker *Harvey D. Goulder,* built in Lorain as hull 342. Full speed in calm weather was 12 miles an hour, typical for ships of her size and era.[11]

Between the hatches, strong traverse girders called arch girders extended around the sections, thus eliminating the needed for stanchions and clearing the holds for easier and quicker unloading. This was especially important to open operating space for the clamshell buckets common at the mill docks. For the same ease of unloading, the spar deck was kept clear of deckhouses or any other obstructions. Speed and efficiency ruled over all.

A new feature of the ship was the forward observation cabin directly under the wheelhouse.[12] It was designed expressly for guest use.[13] It wasn't uncommon to carry special guests of the company during summer trips.

A double bottom ran the length of the ship between the fore and aft peak bulkheads. Side tanks ran up to deck level. When running light, the tanks could carry water as ballast. This is still a common design feature for lakers today.

The builders' prints for the *Joseph Sellwood*, hull 340, and *Loftus Cuddy*, hull 341, were nearly identical to the *Henry B. Smith*, hull 343. All three were built by American Ship Building Company in 1906.

HISTORICAL COLLECTIONS OF GREAT LAKES/BOWLING GREEN STATE UNIVERSITY

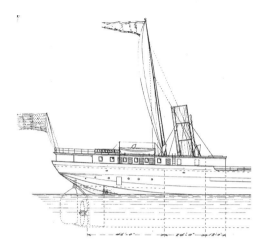

Aft diagram for the *Sellwood/Cuddy* shows the distinct sterns of the new breed of lakers.

HISTORICAL COLLECTIONS OF GREAT LAKES/BOWLING GREEN STATE UNIVERSITY

A short steel forecastle was on the upper deck forward. Cabins for the first and second mates, quartermasters and watchmen were on the portside under the forecastle deck. The owner's staterooms were on the opposite side. A large observation room and the captain's quarters were on the forecastle deck above. The wheelhouse was on the deck above, topped by an open bridge.

The large steel deckhouse aft contained the engineer's quarters, galley and separate dining rooms for the crew, owners and officers, as well as various crew berths. Two metal lifeboats were kept on top of the deckhouse. Two electric generators in the engine room powered her electric lights. Two steel masts, one forward and one aft, were used for signaling as well as mounting running lights. Typical auxiliary machinery included ballast pumps, sanitary pumps, deck pumps, feed and fire pumps, among others.

Both steam steering engines, main and emergency, were located on the main deck aft of the deckhouse. They moved the rudder directly via a toothed quadrant connected to the rudder stock. Steering control came from tele-motors from the wheel in the pilothouse, wheel on the open bridge above or emergency wheel aft. The systems were independent, so the loss of one didn't impact the operation of the other. Both steam systems were typically kept powered while the ship was moving

While improvements at the Soo Locks greatly increased capacity, it never kept up with demand.

and a change-over could be accomplished in seconds by a simple crank arrangement in the wheelhouse.[14]

The steamer was named for Henry Bloomfield Smith, president of the Michigan Pipe Company of Bay City, Michigan. The company made wooden pipes until 1955, selling them all over the world for use in mines, irrigation projects, factories and as gas lines. Wood pipes were lighter and cheaper than iron, could withstand great pressure and were especially adapted to use in chemical plants where iron pipes might become quickly corroded. The company's heyday was during World War II when wooden pipes were in great demand because of a shortage of steel.

Although his primary job was with the pipe company, Smith was also chief officer of the National Bicycle Company. Back in the early 1900s, the country was riding the crest of a cycling craze and National Bicycle Company was "hanging 10," riding the very crest of the wave, as surfers would later say. Crack riders considered it to be one of the best brands in the country. Reputedly

The new *Henry B. Smith* hits the water for the first time.

many world records were broken by National riders and it enjoyed international fame.[15]

Smith was also the vice president of the Smith Steamship Company of Bay City, Michigan. The Smith Steamship Company was one of 13 concerns owned or managed by Hawgoods. His wife, Mary, officially christened the new steamer at the launching at the American Ship Building Company yard in Lorain.

Remarkably there is some confusion regarding the namesake of the ship, some sources claiming she was in honor of Henry Bentley Smith (1849-1918), a prominent lumberman who was managing owner of the Ludington Woodenware Company in Ludington, Michigan. The company manufactured veneer dishes as used by grocery stores for butter and lard, etc., as well as clothespins and mop handles, thus gaining the nickname the "pin mill." Smith was a self-made man. After a stint in the Civil War as a private in an Ohio artillery battalion, he went to a local business school, worked in the merchandising and mill trade around Saginaw, briefly ran a small shipping line from Ludington to Pentwater and finally obtained a strong financial interest in the Ludington mill. The mill moved to Vermont in 1914, when local stocks of hardwood were exhausted.[16]

A more colorful claim is that the boat was named for the H.B. Smith Company owned by Hezekiah B. Smith, a New Englander who later moved to New Jersey with his mistress, Earline. Perhaps half a bubble off level, as the old surveyors would say, he was fond of riding around town in a sulky, pulled by a moose![17] All considered, I like the third explanation best. Never let truth get in the way of a good story.

At one time, Hawgoods (also often called the Acme Transit Company) managed one of the largest fleets on the lakes. The company started in 1881 with schooners and wooden steamers, moving into modern steel freighters as technology changed.

It was common during this period for independent vessel owners like Hawgoods to organize ships into small, sometimes even one-vessel corporations like the Smith Steamship Company. This greatly limited potential liability in the event of a disastrous loss and was considered smart business. However, as part of reorganizing in late 1911, all the fleets were merged into the Acme Transit Company and four of their steamers were sold to meet debts. At this point the *W.A. Hawgood*, *A.H. Hawgood*, *H.A. Hawgood* and *W.R. Woodford* left the company.

The firm collapsed in 1916 and was forced into liquidation following revelations of stock manipulation and receiving secret commissions (aka kickbacks) from the American Ship Building Company for placing orders.[18]

Regardless of the company's eventual demise, fleet boats had black hulls with low white forecastles and white cabins. Older boats had completely black stacks while newer ones had a dark red "H" on a black stack.

The *Smith* was a well-known ship on the lakes, especially in the Lake Superior iron ports. In August 1906, she carried the largest cargo of coal ever hauled to Superior. The 10,731 tons was 31 tons more than the previous record. Instead of Captain Owen, however, she was under the command of Captain Balfour, presumably a relief master.[19]

The old sailors said "they built 'em by the mile and just cut 'em off when they wanted."

The *Smith* had a largely uneventful career, devoid of any serious accidents or damage. In the summer of 1913, she ran aground in the St. Marys River near the Soo, but was freed after a couple of days without injury. Running the river is always a navigational challenge, even for today's freighters equipped with Star Wars electronic course-keeping technology. A century ago it was strictly by compass and eyeball. Add in fog, blinding snow or rain and it was truly difficult.[20]

Valued at $338,000, the *Smith* was insured for $325,000 and carried $30,000 in iron ore on her last trip. *Beeson's Marine Directory*, the bible of Great Lakes shipping, considered her to be "one of the staunchest steel vessels on the lakes." That she would go missing with her entire crew was thought inexplicable.

Life on the *Smith*

Captain James Owen was born in 1858 in Brockville, Ontario, in the Thousand Islands region of the St. Lawrence River. He apparently had no particular family connections to the water since his father worked for the Grand Truck Railway of which the city was an important terminus. It seems that he was bitten by the wanderlust bug at age 16; he and a group of local boys left home for Bay City, Michigan, and the promise of more exciting work than they could find in humdrum Brockville. It didn't take him long to take a job on a boat and he never looked back. Old-timers remembered that when he did steam past Brockville at the helm of a boat, he always saluted the old town with a series of long whistle blasts. After the loss of the *Smith*, folks remembered him as a typical sailor, brusque, blunt and outspoken, but also very generous. He never turned down anyone with a worthy cause needing financial support.[21]

Captain Owen took command of the *Smith* when she came out of the shipyard in 1906. His previous ship was the 440-foot *Edwin F. Holmes,* launched in 1904, which he also brought out of the yard for Acme/Hawgood. Unlike the *Smith,* the *Holmes* had hatches on 24-foot centers, reflecting just how quickly vessel design was changing.[22]

Captain James Owen

The *Holmes* was certainly a well-built ship and, perhaps more importantly, lucky at surviving not only the infamous 1913 storm, but also the 1905 stem-winder. The 1905 storm wrecked or damaged 29 ships with the loss of 39 lives. The full ferocity of the storm struck on November 28 as the *Holmes* was upbound on Lake Huron with coal for Duluth. By the 30th she was past the locks at the Soo and smashing hard into the pile-driver seas. On December 1, Captain Owen brought her in under Duluth's Aerial Bridge, battered but unbroken.

Fast forward to the November 6-11, 1913, storm. By the time it finally blew itself out, nine modern steel vessels foundered with all hands and another 32 were damaged to various degrees. Most important, roughly 250 people lost their lives, most of them sailors now resident in Davy Jones' locker.

The *Smith* fighting through thick ice in Whitefish Bay.

The *Holmes*, still sailing under a lucky star, was caught downbound on Lake Huron on November 9, 1913. The huge waves battered her relentlessly and screaming winds tore at her soul, but the tough ship and crew fought on, eventually safely reaching port.

She continued in the ore, coal and grain trades, changing names several times as she changed ownership. Eventually she ended her sailing days as a cement carrier for the Huron Cement Company under the moniker *J.B. Ford*. She was withdrawn from service in 2008.[23]

Clearly James Owen was a captain in whom the managers had great confidence.[24] After all he was senior captain in the fleet and a veteran master with 30 years of experience in sail and steam, considered to be an outstanding mariner. After the loss of the *Smith,* it became popular for writers to give him nicknames like "Laughing Jimmy Owen," since he reputedly always laughed at the roughest weather, or "Dancing Jimmy Owen" in that as soon as he made port he always headed for the neighborhood dance halls to waltz the night away with the local belles. In point of fact, there is no evidence of such questionable behavior traits in the captain at all. Masters of big new lakers were trustworthy seamen, not seagoing adventurers and gadabouts. Captaining a laker was serious business for serious sailors, at least during the sailing season.

He was also unusual in that in 1908 he reportedly married Mary Ella Cutting, the cook on the *Smith*. Her mother and sisters called her "Pet." At 51 she was a year younger than her husband. Given their ages, it was a childless marriage.

There is an alternate version that when the boats stopped running in the winter, he lived with Captain Alex Begg and his wife, Mary Ella Cutting Begg. After Captain Begg's death in 1906, Captain Owen married Mary Ella and the pair moved to the Cleveland area.[25]

As the true devastation of the terrible 1913 storm became evident and the whereabouts of the *Smith* were unknown, Ella made daily trips from their home in Geneva, 50 miles east of Cleveland, to the Hawgood offices in a desperate quest for news. The terrible end of the *Smith* and her crew soon became plain when the wreckage came ashore.

The Season

The bulk freighters on the lakes follow a predictable rhythm, loading ore on Lake Superior, hauling it down to the mill ports, perhaps holding some more at the Soo Locks, waiting for their turn at the unloaders, then back up for more ore. While speed on the open water was important, it wasn't the speed seen at an automobile race track but rather the constant grind of movement, never stopping unless absolutely necessary. Passing up or down at Detroit, for example, the mail boat, *J.W. Westcott,* ran alongside to pick up and receive mail and small supplies, something still done today. Sometimes even a crewman left or joined the ship the same way. In the Soo, supplies were loaded aboard by tug rather than having the big steamer waste time at a dock. Licensed crewmen were encouraged to stay aboard for the season, too. If they did, companies often paid a bonus. It was cheaper to keep a man than have to find a new one!

Captain Owen previously commanded the *Edwin F. Holmes*. She survived the ravages of the 1913 storm.

Losing undue time to weather, storm or fog was often a black mark against a captain. Timid men who didn't make the most of their ships didn't keep command. Then again, captains who ended up aground in a foggy channel or smacking another boat didn't stay employed either. It was a delicate balancing act between reasonable caution and reasonable risk. In measure, it is the same for captains around the world today.

Loading at the iron ports took perhaps five or six hours, depending on the port and how prepared it was for the *Smith*. Bad weather, as she had in Marquette on November 8 and 9 with ore freezing in the pockets, extended the time even more. The ore wasn't the small marble-sized pellets that we see today but the real thing, hunks of rock several inches in diameter or more, making smooth handling more difficult. To make matters worse, it was 40 percent or so waste rock, but the 60 percent iron made it all worthwhile. This was "natural" or "direct shipping ore" that was pure enough to go directly into the furnace. Unloading ran 10 to 12 hours, again port dependent. In either situation it wasn't unusual to arrive late at night and be under way again before morning. Of course, sometimes the ship was forced to wait for other ships ahead of her, adding to a build-up of delays and implied criticism of the captain.

These shots were taken aboard the *Smith* about 1910. Evidently several unidentified passengers were enjoying a lake cruise.

MARQUETTE MARITIME MUSEUM COLLECTION

Whether loading or unloading, the ship's deckhands had the responsibility to open the hatches or close them as required. It was always hard work, made more difficult by the snow and sleet. They were usually supervised by the second mate or boatswain.

Typically there were perhaps 26 crewmen aboard, enough to do the job but no more: Captain Owen plus two mates, a chief engineer and his first and second assistants, a steward and porter (aka cooks), several watchmen/wheelsmen and a boatswain and his men. They stood watch, ate, slept and repeated the cycle as the *Smith* plowed her way through the lakes. Sometimes one or more of the cooks were women, as demonstrated by the story of Captain Owen marrying his cook in 1908, but on the *Smith*'s last trip they were all male. She also appeared to have a crew of 26 on the final trip although post-wreck reports show only 24 names. Such discrepancies are not uncommon. Crewmen can come and go, perhaps quitting for a perceived slight from an officer or due to illness. The final number wasn't always communicated with the front office.

This class of laker didn't have fore and aft passageways below decks, an innovation that would come about in much later ship design. Such a route was vital during heavy weather when waves regularly sweep over the open weather or spar deck. Considering that the officers lived and mostly worked forward and the crew aft, getting back and forth safely was important. Remember, the galley was aft so if the pilothouse crew wanted to eat, it meant a quick run on the open weather deck. Some freighters rigged a long safety line between the forward house and aft house. A man could clip himself to the line and in theory be prevented from being washed off into  the lake. Whether the *Smith* regularly used one or not is unknown. None show up in period photographs.

Although metallic stations and wire rope "fence rails" ran along both sides of the deck, they were only marginally effective in keeping men from being washed overboard by green water. Sailing was a dangerous business.

Navigational instruments were primitive by today's standards. A big compass in the wheelhouse binnacle swung by an adjuster to compensate for the steel hull of the boat, a pair of binoculars, clock, barometer, a lead line to measure water depth, taffrail log to determine

More posing in the ring. Again, identities are unknown.

MARQUETTE MARITIME MUSEUM COLLECTION

Again identities are unknown, but it is thought Captain Owen is on the right.

MARQUETTE MARITIME MUSEUM COLLECTION

distance run in a given time period, current light list, charts and Great Lakes Pilot books were all tools of the deck officer's trade.

Communication with the engine room was via a Chadburn or engine room telegraph. This was a large mechanical device with a dial and two indicators (one with a large handle attached). One telegraph was on the bridge and the second in the engine room. The dial was divided into the various speeds, such as "all ahead full," "all ahead half," "finished with engines," "all astern full," "all astern half" and so forth. The captain signals a command by adjusting his handle, which sounds an alert bell in the engine room. The engineer sets the engine speed and signals back to the bridge, where it is indicated on a lower portion of the dial confirming his receipt of the order. A brass speaking tube also provided a method of verbally communicating with the engineer.

The rear of the wheelhouse had a large chart table complete with pencils, dividers, parallel rules to plot a course and numerous drawers to hold extra charts. Of course, the charts all had recommended up- and downbound courses printed on them, but they weren't required to be followed. Captains had considerable navigation autonomy. An electric lamp was placed to illuminate the table. Binoculars or a brass telescope were kept in a wooden case mounted on the forward bulkhead. A knotted cord hanging down from the ceiling activated the steam whistle.

The wheel was centered just behind the forward pilothouse windows. A tall stool was often used by the wheelsman to perch on during long open water runs. A small chair with high legs was available for the captain, normally on the port side of the bridge. The wheel didn't control the rudder directly, but rather it actuated a steering engine in the stern, which provide the power to turn the rudder as needed. Depending on the direction of travel and sea conditions, wave force on the rudder could be considerable.

Crew relaxing behind the deckhouse.

It could be said that the engine room was the heart of the boat. The brains may have been forward in the wheelhouse, but the power was deep in the stern, in the netherworld of the engineer. The fire room and engine room were poorly lit and could only be reached via steep and narrow metal frame stairs. It wasn't an area for tourists. The fire hold was dominated by two huge Scotch boilers set side by side running fore and aft.[26]

Each had either one or two small fire doors to access the firebox and grates. The coal passer's job was to feed the twin flame-belching beasts at the direction of the fireman, not just tossing shovelfuls of coal randomly into the firebox, but placing it exactly where needed. The fireman had the more difficult and expert job of raking out the clinkers (unburned impure lumps of coal) with a long steel rake making sure that the grates were clear for better combustion, which meant more power. The added power was vital in a storm.

The crew was well fed on the *Smith,* but mealtime was not an occasion for a leisurely repast. The men ate in the mess room next to the galley, sitting at stools fastened around a long narrow table. Men going on watch ate first and quickly. A second group followed, the men coming off watch arriving hungry and tired. The food was plain but good and filling, with never a man turned away hungry.

In sum there was nothing romantic about the *Smith*. She was a working ship in a difficult and demanding trade, typical of perhaps a hundred others sailing the lakes.

CHAPTER 3

When the Lakes Ran Wild

As Great Lakes sailors know, the worst time to be on the water is November. When the Gales of November come calling, smart sailors are snug in a pub, their fingers curled around a glass of Old Overcoat or like libation. They aren't out battling storm and gale for one more load of red iron ore. The dead hulls of too many lakers, sail and steam, wood, iron and steel, litter Davy Jones' Locker for that!

Most folks are familiar with Sebastian Junger's national best-seller *Perfect Storm*, about three powerful low pressure areas slamming together off the New England coast in late October 1991, causing the loss of the fishing boat *Andrea Gail* with all of her crew. The storm generated 120-mph winds and 100-foot seas. The region in which the boat sank is notorious for storm driven shipwrecks. For example, in the locale where the *Andrea Gail* foundered, four fishing vessels sank, with the loss of 11 lives, during a three-week period in the winter of 1998-99. The Great Lakes, though, are just as deadly.[1]

From November 6 to 11, 1913, the Great Lakes had its own perfect storm, destroying far more than a single small fishing boat. When the waters finally calmed, 19 vessels were completely wrecked and 52 damaged. Fifteen of the lost vessels were steamers, representing a loss of more than $7 million, and remember that this was 1913 when a dollar had real value. Nine of the ships, all steel freighters, were lost with all hands. Ships are still missing, just swallowed whole by the lakes. The loss of life was equally horrific with an estimated 256 sailors killed in what many historians consider the worst storm to ever strike the lakes. Clearly the great Storm of 1913 was a hellbender of epic proportions. No other storm is comparable in terms of pure destruction. The November storms in 1905 and 1940 were each deadly to ships and crews, but only the 1913 storm cut through the lakes with such fatal force that a century later we still stand in awe!

The Lake Carriers' Association, the trade organization for the commercial carriers, later summed up the tragedy in their *1914 Annual Report* stating, "No lake master can recall in all his experience a storm of such unprecedented violence with such rapid changes in the wind and its gusts of such fearful speed! Storms ordinarily of that velocity do not last over four or five hours, but this storm raged for 16 hours continuously at an average velocity of 60 mph, with frequent spurts of 70 and over.

"Obviously with a wind of such long duration, the seas that were made were such that the lakes are not ordinarily acquainted with. The testimony of masters is that the waves were at least 35 feet high and followed each other in quick succession, three waves ordinarily coming right after another.

"They were considerably shorter than the waves that are formed by an ordinary gale. Being of such height and hurled with such force and such rapid succession, the ships must have been subjected to incredible punishment."[2]

The National Oceanographic and Atmospheric Administration (NOAA) (aka the Weather Bureau), in their centennial anniversary re-evaluation of the storm, described it thusly (in classic weather-speak): "The storm of November 1913 began as two separate weather systems. A rather weak low pressure system tracked east across the southern United States from November 6 to 8. At the same time, a secondary low pressure system and associated Arctic cold front moved south out of Canada and approached the Upper Great Lakes the morning of November 7th. The air behind the Arctic front was very cold for early November, with temperatures plunging into the single digits across the Northern Plains. Strong southwest winds dampered up in advance of the low pressure system while a strong northwest wind developed behind it.

"On the morning of November 9th, the southern storm system began to intensify over northern Virginia as the Arctic front pushed southeast through the Ohio Valley. The central pressure dropped to 29.10 inches and absorbed the weaker system approaching from the north. As the much colder air fed into the system, the storm began backing to the north-northwest towards its cold air supply, becoming a meteorological monster, growing and feeding on the moisture from the Atlantic and mixing with the Arctic cold across the Great Lakes.

"By the evening of November 9th, the storm deepened to a very intense central pressure of approximately 28.60 inches (969 millibars) as it tracked north-northwest to eastern Lake Erie. At the same time, strong Arctic high pressure (30.54 inches) was approaching northwest Minnesota. The proximity of the two weather systems resulted in strengthening of the pressure gradient between them, producing a prolonged and intense wind across the Great Lakes. The storm finally began to weaken on November 10th and shifted to the St. Lawrence Valley on November 11th.

"Few wind reports are available from the lakes themselves but hourly observations are available at the ports downwind of the lakes. Lake Huron suffered the greatest losses during the storm and winds measured downwind of the lake at Port Huron, Michigan, increased to 50 to 60 mph during the afternoon and persisted until almost midnight. Winds were even stronger on Lake Erie with speeds of 50-70 mph with gusts near 85 mph."[3]

Considering the relationship of the old Weather Bureau to the Storm of 1913, it is an odd coincidence that the bureau really got its start on the Great Lakes in 1870. After a series of storms sank literally hundreds of ship on the lakes, President Grant, through Congress, established the bureau with the mission to "provide for taking meteorological observations at the military stations

Period Weather Bureau maps tracked the storm's approach.
NOAA

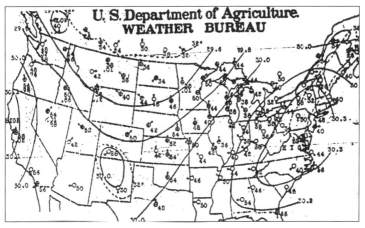
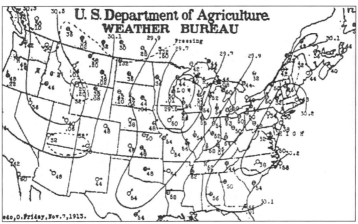
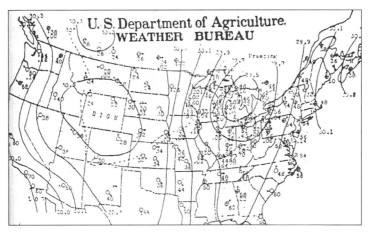

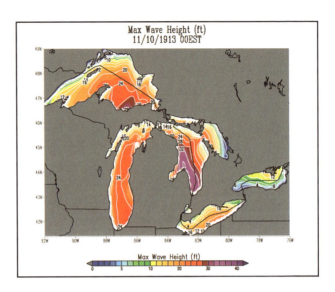

These new NOAA computer models show the intensity of the 1913 storm at midnight on the 10th.
NOAA

in the interior of the continent and at other points in the States and Territories … and for giving notice on the northern (Great) Lakes and on the seacoast by magnetic telegraph and marine signals, of the approach and force of storms." Feeling that solid military discipline was needed in the new agency, it was placed under the direction of the U.S. Army Signal Corps. Its first moniker was the Division of Telegrams and Reports for the Benefit of Commerce.

The first forecasts for the eastern U.S. were issued in 1870, but only for a 24-hour period. It wasn't long before additional stations were brought into the system, including those in the Caribbean, which allowed tracking Atlantic storms, very important for eastern seaboard communities.

In 1890, the organization moved to the Department of Agriculture and pure civilian control. As reflective of the state of the science, forecasts remained vague. All forecasts were issued from the Washington, D.C., office based on the massive flow of data from field stations. This remained problematic for many years, especially since the huge amount of raw data to be manually organized and interpreted invariably delayed the issuance of timely forecasts. And the more data that they received, the more time was needed to process, delaying things even more!

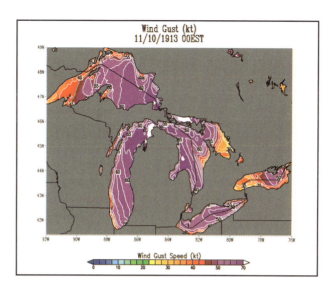

Central control by the government in Washington is always a hard thing to kill.

Radio or "wireless" would have been a great method of warning ships of the coming 1913 storm as well as providing current condition information, but very few ships were equipped with such new technology. Without wireless, all that captains "knew" about the weather was what they could see with their own eyes, interpreting it through experience and whatever forecast was available when they left port. On the open lakes, they were on their own. In their 1914 publication *Important Events in Radio Telegraphy*, the U.S. Department of Commerce, Bureau of Navigation made a strong case for wireless, stating, "November 1913, Great Lakes storms destroyed 19 vessels, none of which were equipped with wireless. All vessels having radio apparatus installed received warning of the coming storm and sought safety."

Weather forecasters weren't asleep but saw the system developing and telegraphed warnings to all Great Lakes ports. By Friday morning November 7, storm-warning flags were up at all the official stations. They did little good. Freighter captains generally ignored them, reasoning, "It's November. Storms are expected, and it's our job to drive through." They looked at it, at least in the beginning, as just another storm, nothing different from so many others. In hindsight, this wasn't as cavalier an attitude as it might appear.

In fact, storms on the Great Lakes are just part of normal business and masters are expected to punch on through the expected fall gales without undue delay. The big iron ships make money by delivering cargo on time and not by hiding in port when the gales of November snort. This outlook was especially true in 1913.

The 1913 storm also devastated land-based activities. Road and rail traffic was paralyzed, telephone, telegraph and power lines ripped down by the screaming wind. Snow and ice shut down rail lines, marooning thousands of people. Thundering waves washed away docks and boathouses and factory smokestacks blew down. What happened ashore was only a pale reflection of the destruction afloat. Waves heaped up to heights that some captains claimed reached 30 feet or more. Banshee winds screamed at 90 miles an hour! Heavy snow smothered visibility, making lookouts useless. Steep waves piled onto bows, sending great deluges of water into wheelhouse windows, blinding captains and wheelsmen to what was happening beyond. Compasses swung wildly in their binnacles as wave after wave hammered into the hull.

In an age before radar, the ships were literally running blind in the storm, trusting to the gods that there was nothing ahead of them in their patch of whirling white. Every vessel on the lakes was in desperate straits during the 1913 storm. It was only a case of how desperate.

Determining the true measure of a storm is always difficult, and from a writer's perspective, the temptation to increase the size or the waves and force of the wind is always present. I've tried my best to present the facts of the prevailing weather as best I find them. In some cases conditions were based on those recorded by official weather stations, others by the crews caught in the center of the maelstrom of the 1913 storm.

All that said, in 2013 NOAA took another look at the 1913 storm using the best modeling techniques of the Weather Research and Forecast (WRF) modeling system and the NOAA Great Lakes Environmental Research Laboratory to produce a more detailed and accurate look at the storm. Included also was the Donelan Wave Model to reconstruct true sea state, including significant wave height, dominant wave period and wind-wave direction. Peak wave height was included to characterize the worst observed conditions.

Certainly in any study of this kind, a number of sources of error can creep into the calculations, so perfection is not possible. But that said, as the study stated, "even a less-than-perfect simulation affords important context into what happened and when."

This is especially true of a 100-year retrospective. The resulting study looked at the Storm of 1913 as two storms. The first or "pre-storm" struck Lake Superior and Lake Michigan on November 7 and 8. It was formidable in its own right. Storm-force winds accompanied by heavy snow including lake-effect snow squalls, freezing spray and high seas savaged both lakes, causing a number of shipping problems.

The second storm, sometimes referred to as the "White Hurricane," struck on November 9-11. It resulted from an atypical atmospheric phasing of the "pre-storm" to the north with the developing storm over the southeast United States. The resulting "weather bomb" over the eastern Great Lakes spawned hurricane-force winds, blinding snow squalls, freezing spray and massive waves over the Great Lakes.

As the storm hammered the lakes, winds dramatically increased with gusts greater than 80 mph common. The gusts exceeded hurricane force (more than 74 mph) predicted by the modeling for extended time over lakes Huron, Erie, Superior and Michigan.

<u>Hurricane-Force Wind Periods</u>
Lake Huron – 10 hours
Lake Superior – 20 hours
Lake Michigan – 13 hours
Lake Erie – 16 hours

Modeling waves during the storm was a critical part of the overall simulation. It is critical to understand that all waves are not created equal. Rather, the size of waves sampled across a given time (say an hour) will differ across a known spectrum of heights. To help differentiate waves, according to the simulation, meteorologists and mariners describe "significant waves" as the average of the largest one-third (33%) and "maximum waves" as the average of the highest one-twentieth (5%)."

For example, if the average wave over an hour sample is 5 feet with a wave period of 8 seconds ... a "significant wave" will be 7.8 feet and will occur once every 40 seconds, and a "maximum wave" will be 8.9 feet and will occur once every 2-3 minutes. "Maximum waves" are generally the worst conditions boats will encounter regularly. A wave period is the time it takes two successive crests to pass a given point.[4]

While the NOAA scientists were looking at the data in a very scientific way, it is worth remembering that old Great Lakes legend of the "Three Sisters," a phenomenon claimed to occur in Lake Superior when a series of three waves form that are a third bigger than the normal waves. What makes the Three Sisters so deadly is that the second wave rolls over a ship's deck before the first wave washes clear. The third wave adds to the pile of water, overloading the deck, and down she goes. The Three Sisters was suggested by some folks as one of the early explanations for the loss of the *Edmund Fitzgerald*.

A quick look at the wave data generated by the simulation is extremely illuminating.

Saturday, November 8
10 p.m. – At end of Storm 1, Lake Huron waves 6-8 feet

Sunday, November 9
10 a.m. – Lake Superior waves diminishing, Lake Huron 8-12 feet
    4 p.m. – All lakes waves increasing
        "Bomb" approaches eastern Lake Erie
    6 p.m. – Lake Huron maximum waves 24 feet
        Argus lost vicinity Pointe aux Barques
    8 p.m. – Rapidly building waves on Lake Huron
        <u>Sunk or aground</u>
        Howard M. Hanna Jr., John A. McGean, Isaac M. Scott, Hydrus
        Wind gusting 80 mph, maximum waves 28 feet
        Next four hours deadliest in Great Lakes maritime history
  10 p.m. – Maximum waves 36 feet
  11 p.m. – <u>Sunk or aground</u>
        Charles Price, Regina; D.O. Mills aground at Harbor Beach

12 p.m. – Storm peaks over Lake Huron
  Winds at 75-80 mph, maximum waves 36 feet
  Sunk or aground
  Wexford, James Carruthers; Matoa aground Pointe aux Barques

Monday, November 10
  2 a.m. – Storm center moves to vicinity London, Ontario
    Highest winds lakes Erie, Superior, northern Michigan
  6 a.m. – Winds 80-plus mph
    Maximum waves 36 feet at Pictured Rocks Nat'l Lakeshore
    Maximum waves Lake Erie 22 feet
  8 a.m. – Maximum waves near Munising, Lake Superior 38 feet
  10 a.m. – Hurricane force southwest winds on Lake Erie
    Maximum 24-foot waves near Buffalo
    Sunk or aground
    Lightship No. *82* lost, Steamer *Sylvania* reports "massive" waves near Whitefish Point
  12 p.m. – Decreasing winds and waves Lake Superior
    32-foot waves vicinity Marquette
  6 p.m. – Waves still high, but decreasing
    Low near Toronto

Tuesday, November 11
  12 a.m. – Waves begin to weaken

Of all the lakes, Huron bore the brunt of the attack. Over the southern part of the lake there was a dramatic ratcheting up of wind speed during the afternoon and evening of Sunday, November 9, escalating from 52 mph at 1 p.m. to 80-plus mph eight hours later. The simulation verified that survivor claims of 90 mph were quite possible.

The scientists consider the resulting modeling to be remarkably accurate considering that by modern standards there weren't a lot of ground observations and there were no upper air (balloon) or satellite observations. Models predicting surface pressure conditions came very close to actual observed conditions, the mark of a good simulation.

Likewise the predicted storm location and central pressure are very close, providing additional confidence that wind and wave conditions extrapolated from the simulation are representative of what mariners actually encountered 100 years ago.[5] To the best extent that I could, I used the NOAA modeling data in describing wind and wave conditions unless I had what I considered to be inherently more accurate observations.

Lake Erie

Although Lake Erie wasn't in the epicenter of the storm, it suffered its own share of disasters, the worst being the loss of Lightship *82* with all hands. She was barely a year out of her builder's yard, Racine-Truscott-Shell Lake Boat Company at Muskegon, Michigan. As a class, lightships are built to be virtually unsinkable by wave, wind or collision. On the small side (lightships were never large), she measured 95 feet in length and 21 feet in beam. The tough steel hull was capped by a whaleback forecastle deck with a single mast for her lantern roughly amidships and a small mizzen mast with a boom on her stern. The sail on the mizzen could help steady her up during wind, making her ride more comfortable for the small crew. Comfort, however, was a relative term in a lightship. A tall smokestack was abaft the lantern mast. An underpowered 90-horsepower steam engine provided capability of getting under way in an emergency, but not enough power for maneuvering in anything but calm weather. Typically the lightship would be towed by a tug if the ship needed to move off station.

The duty of a lightship was always to stay in position to warn ships of a close-by hazard, or in some instances, the critical point for a harbor entrance. It was a dangerous job. A fierce storm could blow the lightship into the deadly reef or other hazard. During fog a big freighter could literally run her down as she was "following" the mournful bleats of the lightship fog signal. The lightship's only defense against this was the strength of her construction. Given her design, she was literally a ship killer, better able to withstand a collision than the ship bearing down on her. During their years of use nationwide, there were 150 collisions between lightships and other vessels. Only five resulted in the loss of the lightship. Regardless of the odds, standing watch on one during a fog and hearing the blasts of fog horns all around you, some apparently bearing directly for you, was unnerving! The most well-known collision occurred on May 15, 1934, when the RMS *Olympic* (sister ship of the *Titanic*) ran down the lightship *Nantucket* with the loss of eight of the 11 lightship crewmen aboard.

For a while lightships were popular with the Lighthouse Bureau, peaking in 1909 with 56 in all American waters. Twenty were used on the Great Lakes in 18 locations between 1891 and 1970.[6]

Lightship No. 82 was lost off Buffalo with all hands.

In terms of habitability for crews, lightships were not much different from steamers of the period with some exceptions. Bunks were slanted inward to keep the men from being rolled out from vessel motion during violent weather. Lightships tended to "roll their guts out" during any sea condition worse than flat calm. To help fight the crushing boredom, a normal lighthouse library chest was aboard. The men had their sea chest for clothing and personal gear storage. While the galley was small, it was well-equipped and the men took turns cooking. Eating, though, was often difficult when vessel motion kicked up. Just keeping plates on the table was challenging. Most mess tables had wood edging to keep the crockery from smashing to the deck. Wet tablecloths helped, too. The crew in some lightships even drilled holes in the table top and inserted small pegs, constructing a little fence around every piece of tableware. But in the most extreme conditions nothing really worked.

Sitting atop the lantern mast was the reason for Lightship No. *82*'s existence, a cluster of three 300 mm oil lanterns on a hoisting sleeve allowing them to be lowered for maintenance and raised at night. A steam-driven 10-inch fog whistle was also ready when needed. The back-up was a hand-operated bell.

Crewing on a lightship was considered by most to be miserable duty. Manning a shore lighthouse was heaven by comparison. On land you could take walks, have visitors or maybe go to town. Even if stationed on an isolated tower, like Rock of Ages at Isle Royale, the bloody tower didn't move, dancing around like a thing possessed every time there was a hint of a breeze. Even longtime sailors often suffered terrible bouts of seasickness from the unusual gut-wreching movement of a lightship. One lightship captain is reputed to have remarked, "If it weren't for the shame of it, I'd rather go to the state prison."[7]

The Lighthouse Bureau accepted No. *82* from the builder on July 12, 1912, placing her on station, 13 miles off the entrance to Buffalo Harbor on August 3. She was anchored in position by four 4-ton mushroom anchors secured to her keelson with huge chains. She wasn't going anywhere.

Six men made up her crew: Captain Hugh M. Williams, Mate Andrew Leahy, Chief Engineer Charles W. Butler, Assistant Engineer Cornelius Leahy and crewmen Peter Mackey and William Jensen. The mate and assistant engineer were brothers.

The 1913 storm hammered Lake Erie hard, especially the south shore. Eight-foot-high snowbanks made roads impassable, power and telegraph/telephone lines knocked down, railroads overwhelmed by the drifts on the tracks. No. *82* took the full brunt of the storm.

The last moments of No. *82* can only be conjectured. As with many of the storm losses, there were no survivors and no witnesses. Lake Erie is well-known for the ferocity of her storms, driven in part by the shallow water and propensity to build large waves quickly. The northwesterly seas smashed into the lightship with devastating force, hammering her again and again. With her short anchor scope she had nowhere to go, unable to ride the waves as a normally anchored ship could and with her weak engine couldn't hope to lessen the pounding by steaming into the seas. The crew could only ride it out and pray.

Lightship No. 82 after salvage.

Seas flooding over her deck swept it clear of gear, secured or not. Water pouring into the cabins and flooding deep down to the bilge slowly overwhelmed her pumps straining to keep up. For a while she survived, but barely. When the wind shifted northeast, a vicious cross chop slammed her one way, then another, as the seas competed for the pleasure of destroying the plucky little lightship. The strain on her chains was tremendous. The wind increased in strength, shrieking with devil-spewed venom, forcing her over on her beam ends with waves tearing away her wood cabins. Swinging north, the wind blasted her even harder, sending the lantern mast crashing into the sea with the stack following.

The crew must have huddled below waiting for the inevitable end. Her lifeboat was long gone, swept away by the seas. Their life jackets were useless, at most allowing a body to be found.

At the height of the storm, the mooring cables tore loose and No. *82* was sent off into the darkness. Waves continued to tear her apart. Waterlogged and hopeless, she dove for bottom, her fight finished. The little ship and her six-man crew were wiped off the lake.

In the flood of disastrous storm reports, she wasn't missed until 3 a.m. November 11 when the steamer *Champlain* passed her station but didn't see her. The *Champlain* was badly battered herself, barely making it into Buffalo. Most marine men ignored the fears for the lightship's safety expressed by the steamer's captain.

The schooner-barge *Plymouth* wrecked and was later salvaged in Marquette in 1887.

The locals thought she was just blown off station but soon would turn up. A few days later a "Light Vessel *LV-82*" life jacket washed up on a city beach. It was an ominous sign of what was to come. Soon other wood wreckage proved the loss of the sturdy little lightship. The only direct report of loss was a quick note that Captain Williams scrawled on a piece of wood to his wife. "Good-by Mary, the ship is breaking up fast. Williams." By some accounts his body later washed up on the shore several days later. Others say he was never found. Nearly a year later, the remains of the chief engineer were recovered in the Niagara River, 13 miles distant from the wreck. Reportedly no others were ever found.

The wreck of No. *82* was located the following May, nearly a mile to the northeast of its original station. The entire upper works was destroyed, torn to pieces by the battering waves of Lake Erie. On September 16, 1915, the wreck was raised, rebuilt and returned to service.

The oddest wreck from the storm was the caravel *Santa Maria*, Columbus' flagship. Replicas of the *Niña*, *Pinta* and *Santa Maria* were moored for the winter in Erie, Pennsylvania, when the storm winds arrived. On Sunday, November 9 the blasts blew the small ship off her mooring and onto a sand bar outside the harbor. She was in the city as part of a national tour.

Lake Michigan

Lake Michigan saw the loss of the big 225-foot schooner barge *Plymouth* reputedly off St. Martin Island in the northern lake. The schooner was in tow of the tug *James H. Martin* when the hawser broke in the heaving seas. Desperately fighting for her own life, the tug abandoned the *Plymouth* to her fate, condemning her nine-man crew to death. The newspapers reported the tug arrived in Menominee, Michigan, in sinking condition. There was also the inevitable "message in a bottle." Chris Keenan, a temporary deputy U.S. marshal, on board the *Plymouth* to secure the barge in a legal dispute, was the author. Talk about being in the wrong place at the wrong time; this landsmen truly drew the short straw. Addressed to his wife and children, it reportedly said, "We were left up here in Lake Michigan by McKinnon (captain of the tug). He went away and never even said goodbye. Lost one man yesterday. We have been in storm 40 hours. I felt so bad I had to have another man write for me. I may see you in heaven dear ones. Chris." The bottle was discovered low on the beach 5 miles from Pentwater, on the Michigan side of the lake.

On the 9th, the 319-ton schooner *G.J. Boyce,* bound from Westerville, Ontario, to Chicago with 375,000 feet of lumber and a crew of seven, raced for the harbor entrance in the midst of the storm. Battered by wind and sea, she couldn't keep a course through the breakwaters, so the captain hove to and signaled for a tug to come out and drag her inside. After some delay the tug *Kenosha* came out and put a hawser aboard her, but when she took a strain it broke, leaving the *Boyce* hard driving for a lee shore and certain wreck. Her desperate crew was able to drop her anchors after a frantic effort while the tug ran back in to get a new hawser.

After seeing the drama unfolding from the station lookout tower, the Life-Saving keeper dispatched four surfmen out to her in the surfboat to assist wherever they could. When the tug returned with a new line, Life-Savers and sailors struggled to get it made up, but to no avail. The wind and waves were increasing as the storm reached a peak and getting a line fast was impossible.

Meanwhile the small surfboat returned to the station leaving the four surfmen aboard the beleaguered schooner. The storm continued to rage through the 10th and 11th, finally moderating on the 12th. Freezing water heavily coated the schooner and her deck load of lumber. Incredibly, the anchors held and she survived the tempest. With easier weather a tug assisted by the remainder of the Life-Savers brought the *Boyce* to safety in the harbor.[8]

The passenger and freight steamer *Illinois* fought her own lonely battle with the storm. When Captain John A. Stuffelbeam finally brought her into Chicago three days late, he reported that the tempest struck her Sunday and he was forced to run her into the small bay at South Manitou Island. Since the island has no harbor, he put her stem hard against the beach and kept his engines running for 24 hours to prevent her from being blown broadside to the shore. When the wind and sea moderated a bit, the crew ran a line to a tree as a mooring and safely waited out the storm.[9]

The Life-Saving Crew at Plum Island, Wisconsin, nearly to the end of the Door Peninsula and on the very edge of the infamous "Death's Door Passage," was in an ideal location to render aid to ships in distress. When they received a message that the wooden steamer *Louisiana* was wrecked but in no immediate trouble on Washington Island just to the north, the crew promptly headed out. She was bound for Escanaba and, buffeted by wind and wave, sought shelter in Washington Harbor, eventually consumed by fire to a total loss. On the way to the wreck another message reached the Life-Savers that the big schooner-barge *Halstead* was wrecked on the north side of the island, 8 miles distant.

Since the original *Louisiana* message said they couldn't immediately help the steamer, they headed for the *Halstead* and her endangered crew. By the time they made the 8-mile trek, they found her three-quarters of a mile offshore and dragging quickly for the beach.

When he left the station, the keeper was unsure what the situation would be at the wreck site so he brought both his surfboat and beach apparatus. However the hurricane force winds prevented any attempt to launch the boat, and she was too far off for rescue by a Lyle Gun, regardless of the wind. The Life-Savers could only wait for the *Halstead* to drift closer and pray for a chance to work their magic.

The *Halstead* came on in fits and starts, dragging for a while then fetching up on the reefs until another blast set her heading for the beach again. About 5 a.m. on the 10th, she finally struck hard into a rock pile about 60 feet off shore. The Life-Saving crew quickly had a shotline across her with a whipline hawser-and-breeches buoy following. But before the first man could come ashore, a monstrous wave grabbed the schooner flinging her so far up the beach that the crew could lower a ladder and reach shore without getting wet.[10] This was rescue the easy way.

CHAPTER 4

Huron Moaned

Lake Huron

While all of the Great Lakes were punished by the storm, the worst losses were on Lake Huron. The ships and crews found themselves in the wrong place at the wrong time and paid dearly for it.

As the obliteration of Lake Huron shipping slowly came into focus, every minute seemed to bring news of tragedy. Given the downed telephone and telegraph lines, reports were very slow reaching authorities and newspapers. It was a tortuously slow drip of death.

Rather than try to piece together the loss of vessels in a tight chronological order, first this one sank then that one, etc., I've elected just to boil 'em all up with the same ice fog of confusion that the scene presented to those safe ashore. I also don't treat all shipwrecks as equal, but rather explore some more deeply than others. Many books on the market may cover a reader's "favorite" wreck in greater detail than I do. To a point, this sets the scene for the Lake Superior drama.

Each of the vessels caught in the storm fought her own long battle, some to the death. As the weather witches brewed, Lake Huron was the epicenter of what was, in reality, a freshwater hurricane. The litany of dead ships drones on and on.

The upbound 416-foot Interlake freighter *Argus* with coal, in command of Captain Paul Guetch, broke in two and sank in Lake Huron with the loss of all hands. Many bodies of the crew of 25 eventually washed ashore near Kincardine, Ontario. The wreck was finally discovered in

1972. She was built by Bay Ship Building Company in Lorain in 1903. The downbound *Hydrus*, Captain James Lowe, a sister ship to the *Argus* and also an Interlake freighter, foundered in Lake Huron off Lexington, Michigan, taking her entire crew of 28 with her. She was loaded with iron ore.

The 550-foot freighter *James Carruthers*, the largest freighter in the Canadian fleet, and under Captain William H. Wright, was so new that she was only on her third trip. She was downbound on Lake Huron with wheat from Thunder Bay for Midland on Georgian Bay when storm waves pounded her. It is thought that she capsized. Pitifully few bodies of her crew of 25 were recovered. After her loss, some mariners speculated that her wheat cargo made her ride too high in the water, thus more prone to rolling on her beam ends. Heavy iron ore would have kept her upright, or so their theory went. Their argument made a lot of sense, especially given the storm conditions. Grain is one of the most difficult and dangerous cargoes to carry in bulk. Most grains have an angle of repose (slip angle) of about 20 degrees from horizontal. If the ship rolls more than 20 degrees the cargo will shift, usually resulting in a large list that in turn will drive more and more of the cargo to shift until the ship finally capsizes.

The *James Carruthers* was the largest Canadian freighter on the Great Lakes.

The *Carruthers* was a modern laker in every way. Her builders used the web-and-arch system, freeing her cargo hold of upright stanchions and easing handling through her 31 hatches. Like other freighters of her day, including the *Smith*, hatches were covered with telescoping steel leafs. The cargo hold was divided into five compartments separated by screen (none watertight) bulkheads.

Collision bulkheads were aft of the bow and forward of the engine room. Her 2,400-horsepower triple expansion steam engine was fired by three Scotch boilers, providing sufficient power for 11 mph loaded or 13 mph empty. There is a question as to whether she had a wireless or not. She was built for the St. Lawrence and Chicago Navigation Company.

The *Carruthers* may have been the biggest and brightest star of the Canadian fleet, but Captain Wright was cautious with his new charge. Before leaving Thunder Bay he talked with Captain S.A. Lyons of the steamer *J.H. Sheadle*. Both masters agreed to run down together. A little company isn't a bad thing, especially in an unruly Lake Superior.

The brunt of the storm hit on November 8 while both were in mid-Superior and roughly halfway to the Soo. Quickly locking through, they continued down river with the exception of a quick coaling stop that the *Carruthers* made at Lime Island shortly after midnight on November 9. The popular coaling station was just up river from DeTour and the entrance to Lake Huron.

Both ships continued out into Lake Huron, the *Sheadle* running behind the *Carruthers*. Sometime after dawn the *Carruthers* turned to port, taking a heading to run directly across Lake Huron into Georgian Bay and Midland. She was never seen again, at least afloat.

Her bodies mostly came ashore between Kincardine and Point Clark on the Canadian side of the lake. Among them was her captain, William H. Wright, identified by his huge red mustache. Unlike those from other ships, the *Carruthers* bodies wore life jackets over heavy coats, suggesting that the men had time to prepare to leave the ship. Perhaps the light wheat cargo did shift, providing sufficient time for the captain to order his crew to prepare to leave her.

Adding more to the mystery, residents of Inverhuron, Ontario, reportedly heard a ship's distress whistles and saw rockets offshore. If true and they were fired from the *Carruthers*, she was far off her course for Midland. Whether whistles were heard or rockets sighted during the height of the storm is problematic. But it was their story and they were sticking to it.

Sometimes fate plays strange tricks. The body of an unidentified sailor washed ashore mixed in with the *Price* and *Regina* bodies on the Canadian shore (see pages 62-65). The only unique feature was "J.T." tattooed on his left forearm. The body was battered, but face generally untouched. A scar ran across his nose and leg. An eyetooth was missing, too. His hair was light brown. He had no papers, wallet, rings or anything to lock down his identity. He was duly placed in the Goderich morgue awaiting identification.

When it was clear to all that the *Carruthers* was gone, Thomas Thompson went to Goderich looking for the body of his son John, a crewman on the ill-fated steamer. Hopefully they would at least have his remains back. The one with the tattoo sure looked like his son, given the scars, missing tooth, tattoo and even two disfigured toes. While the hair was wrong, light brown instead of nearly black, the coroner assured him that it was likely caused by immersion in the cold water. Thomas took possession of the body and brought it home to Hamilton, Ontario, for a proper funeral.

Meanwhile, John was reading of his "death" in a Toronto newspaper. In a stroke of luck, he had left the *Carruthers* earlier and signed aboard the steamer *Maple*, waiting out the screaming storm winds safe in port. After reading about the loss of the *Carruthers* in the newspaper, he realized that his family and friends would think him dead, so he saw it as a great opportunity for a prank. Instead of sending a telegram letting them know that he was alive, he just did nothing, taking a slow train to Hamilton to surprise them in person. Even after he arrived in his home city, he didn't immediately head home but visited with a friend first.

In the interim his father had purchased a coffin, readied a grave and held the wake. When John finally wandered home, his mother was ecstatic that her son was safe, but his father was livid. His son's "joke" had cost him dearly; the price of a coffin, open grave and wake expenses were a real financial burden for the less than well-off family. He ordered him out of his house until things blew over.

The faux John Thompson was never identified, but simply returned and buried with other "unknowns" from the storm in Goderich.[1]

The wreck of the *Carruthers* was reportedly located in the 1980s, but this is certainly open to question. Whether a "missing" boat is found or not can be a fascinating saga of intrigue and secrecy. In the modern age, many divers have spent countless hours searching for "virgin" wrecks, ones that previously were undiscovered. In the old days the goal was to find her and strip her of all the "goodies" such as wheel, blocks, compass, crockery and so on. When the "find" was eventually announced, credit was duly awarded but of course it is a much diminished wreck historically than prior to discovery.

So is the *Carruthers* found or not? Good question, eh? But if you were a diver lucky enough to find her, would you tell the world or take your time exploring and photographing it before a host of your web-footed friends overwhelmed her? I'll let you judge.

The 5-year-old Hutchinson freighter *John A. McGean,* under the command of 30-year veteran Captain Chauncey R. Ney, was upbound on Lake Huron with coal from Sandusky for Lake Superior when she smashed into the storm. The 432-foot steamer was last sighted off Tawas, Michigan, before foundering with all hands. As with the *Regina* and *Price*, the lifeless bodies of the crew soon came ashore. Three were lashed to a life raft bearing the name *John A. McGean,* reaching the beach 5 miles south of Goderich, Ontario. The local coroner made the identification only by their clothing. The broken wreck was finally discovered in 1982 by legendary Great Lakes wreck hunter David Trotter. She was built by the American Ship Building Company at Lorain in 1908.

Reputedly Captain Ney had the nickname "Dancing Chauncey" for his skillful navigation of the dance floor while in port. Doubtless he was greatly missed by a fleet of partners.[2] Described as a "jolly good natured fellow

The *Wexford* was another of the 1913 missing ships.

of middle age," he was well-known in Marquette social circles.³ Like similar nicknames given to Captain James Owen after the wreck of the *Smith*, "Dancing Chauncey" was more newspaper hype than fact. But what reporter wants to ignore such a great story?

The 250-foot *Wexford* fought her own desperate combat with a hell-spawned Lake Huron. Like her sister in death, the *Regina,* she was a three-island freighter built in 1883 by Doxford & Sons in the UK, in this instance Sunderland, England. In common parlance she was a tramp steamer, one whose trading routes were dictated by cargo needs rather than a defined route and ports to a schedule. That said, she was intended to trade between England and South America with an occasional foray to the Mediterranean.

Sold to the French in 1890, she was renamed *Elise,* but 23 years later was sold back to the Brits (Western Steamship Company of Toronto) and brought to the Great Lakes. She was soon in Collingwood on Georgian Bay and was given a refit, including boilers and engine. In a most unusual move, she also received her old name.

Over the years she regularly hauled cargoes of miscellaneous package freight and steel rail up to Thunder Bay on western Lake Superior, returning laden with Canadian grain. It was a steady and reliable trade.

Ominously, she also had an unusual amount of accidents. Among them, in August 1913 she damaged 30 to 40 bottom plates after grounding at Lime Island in the lower St. Marys River while refueling. Extensive yard work put her right. Her captain immediately took "sick leave" after the incident. Whether the two events are connected is speculative.

The storm caught her on Lake Superior bound down from Thunder Bay (Fort William/Port Arthur) with a cargo of 96,000 bushels of grain bound for Goderich. It was a miserable trip across Lake Superior, as would be expected. Reaching the Soo she locked through continuing on down river to anchor off DeTour just short of Lake Huron. While she had a crew of only 16, seven passengers were also aboard. Her captain was 24-year-old Bruce Cameron. Recently married, he was considered a stellar hockey player. With his ship safely on the hook, Cameron settled down to wait out the storm.[4]

The crew wasn't strictly male. The stewardess was Grace Wilmott, wife of steward George Wilmott. It was intended to be their last trip before taking a ship home to England.

But ships don't earn their keep hanging around on anchor line, and at the first indication that the storm was over, Captain Cameron hauled chain and steamed into the open lake bound for Goderich. Hindsight is always 20/20; he should have stayed at anchor. Perhaps a more experienced master would not have fallen for the "sucker hole," a colloquial term for a short spate of good weather that "suckers" captains into leaving port just in time for a storm ratcheting back to full force. But whether experience would have kept him anchored is so much idle speculation.

Apparently she was last sighted about 10:30 a.m. on November 9, just north of Port Clark, about 60 miles north of Sarnia, by the 250-foot British steamer *Kaministiquia* on the east shore of the lake. The *Kaministiquia*'s men didn't see any distress signals or other indication that she wasn't in good shape. It wasn't long before the *Kaministiquia* was graced by the full glory of the storm. The *Wexford* would have been hammered at the same time.

From this point, what happened to her is the purest of speculation. One report has her sighted off Goderich through rapidly rolling squalls. If her intention was to enter Goderich Harbour, it was a suicide mission. Getting in meant navigating through a very narrow and poorly lit channel mouth, then running down a long narrow breakwater-lined channel before reaching the comparatively wide inner harbor. Under the blasting winds and monster seas, it was a mission impossible for an experienced captain, let alone a youngster like Cameron.

Perhaps Captain Cameron was trying to lay offshore and wait for daylight. Some folks thought they heard the mournful blasts of a ship's whistle blowing distress during the worst of the storm. One claimant was a grain elevator operator attesting that he heard them before 4 a.m. on November 10. Regardless of what people thought or believed they heard, when daylight came, the lake was empty of the *Wexford*. Where had she gone?

Doubts to her fate were cast aside when the inevitable melancholy flotsam came ashore, including the battered remains of some of her crew. Several bodies were discovered by a farmer near Grand Bend, 30 miles to the south.

The question of her location became one of the great mysteries of the 1913 storm. As time passed, the diving community, including the old hard-hat divers, heard inside rumors of discovery, but of course it was all gossip … maybe.

The only verifiable discovery of the *Wexford* happened on August 25, 2000, when divers investigating an "obstruction" fouling a sport fisherman's gear discovered the long-lost steamer in 75 feet of water. The discovery is especially ironic since a search team with very expensive high-technology side-scan sonar was "mowing the grass" looking for her at the same time, but several miles away. In contrast, the fisherman established the size and shape of his obstruction with a simple $150 depth finder. Divers report her as sitting upright, reputedly in great condition but heavily encrusted in zebra mussels.

The *Jane Miller* and her 31 passengers and crew disappeared on Lake Huron in November 1881.

While finding the wreck at least solved the mystery of location, it didn't explain why she was there; 8.6 miles west northwest of Grand Bend, 32 miles south of Goderich so many miles from where she should have been. All previous evidence placed her somewhere off Goderich, not so very far to the south of the town.

The best conventional wisdom claimed that Captain Cameron hove to off Goderich, likely putting her hooks down to pull the bow into the waves while using her engine to keep steaming ahead, thus stopping the wind and sea from driving her into the beach. Surely if she sank, the wreck must be on the bottom somewhere off the port. This old theory was trashed when divers discovered both anchors still securely tucked into their pockets. Had she used them to hove to, it was likely that the captain would have just run the chains out instead of trying to haul them up when he decided to break for shelter in the St. Clair River. Hauling anchors in storm conditions can be very difficult.

Her engine room telegraph indicated "1/8 ahead," a very slow speed for trying to hold her head into the hammering seas. Reportedly the rudder is missing and both Scotch boilers are intact. Without more information, the role of the lost rudder is speculative at best, but intact boilers suggest a slow sinking with enough time for sufficient cooling as not to explode when the cold lake water hit them. It was common, but not certain, that hot boilers exploded when cold water suddenly flooded them.

The most important clue may be her missing smokestack. Reportedly it isn't on the wreck, although it could be buried nearby in the mud of the bottom or could be miles away, blown off by the grasping gusts of wind well before she finally sank.

Stacks weren't just a convenient way to funnel noxious fumes away from a boat; rather, the steamers needed the draft provided by the stack to function. No stack meant that the boiler fires ceased to burn, steam wasn't produced and the engine became just so much dead weight.

My thought (which is certainly only reasonable speculation) is that she did heave to off Goderich hoping the storm would blow itself out or at least lull a bit, and lost her stack in the screaming wind. Without it, she was doomed. Without power she was forced into the deadly trough of the seas and drifted rapidly southward. Captain Cameron's leaving the telegraph at 1/8 ahead was a meaningless gesture. Perhaps he just forgot in the confusion of the moment. Without draft, the boiler fires went out, thus there was no explosion when she finally sank. Her rudder could have been lost in the deep rolling caused by the towering waves. Regardless of the details of death, she was overwhelmed by the storm and plummeted to the bottom. Whether she tried to launch a lifeboat or not is a moot point since all aboard perished.

The storm also brought up gristly reminders of earlier Georgian Bay shipwrecks. Part of the hull of the small steamer *Jane Miller* washed ashore near Cape Croker, the first piece of the wreck found since she disappeared November 26, 1881, in the midst of a screamer. Considered a true ghost ship of the bay, she vanished with 30 passengers and crew en route from Meaford to Wiarton. Some of the cargo of the 107-foot steamer *J.J.*

Jones also came ashore in the same area. She was lost with all 26 passengers and crew on November 26, 1906, in another gale. But it wasn't only wreckage and cargo found on the beach. The battered remains of a man drowned four years earlier also were disgorged by the thundering seas of the bay.

Many Great Lakes mariners were surprised at the loss not only of the *Wexford,* but *Regina* and *Leafield,* too. They were built for saltwater service, generally thought to be a much more demanding environment than the Great Lakes. The learned mariners pondered how ships designed and built to sail the world's oceans, through typhoon and hurricane, could be overwhelmed by a simple Great Lakes storm.

While any vessel lost with all hands has an element of mystery, the 504-foot *Charles S. Price*, under Captain W.A. Black, was particularly inexplicable. She was last sighted upbound in northern Lake Huron near the Canadian package freighter *Regina*. Both ships were fighting for their lives and apparently winning their struggles. Like much of the new laker fleet, she was built by the American Ship Building Company in Lorain, coming into service in 1910. Her holds were filled with coal.

When the storm finally blew itself out and marine men tried to account for their missing ships, they discovered a large freighter floating upside down north of Fort Gratiot Light at the south end of Lake Huron. There were so many ships unaccounted for that her identity was unknown. What ship was it? Not until a hardhat diver descended on the dead hull was she identified as the *Charles S. Price*. Sometime during the height of the storm she had apparently rolled, killing all 28 of her crew. But there was a survivor, of a kind.

Perhaps acting on intuition or just an overwhelming desire to be home with his family, first assistant engineer Milton Smith resigned his position, leaving the ship in Duluth before the final trip. He was replaced by the unfortunate Mr. Reynolds of Cleveland. Doubtless, Milton Smith's wife and their six young children, the oldest 11, were overjoyed at Smith's decision!

The 249-foot freighter *Regina*.

The *Regina*, a 249-foot Canadian package freighter with young Captain E.H. McConkey, was also lost and presented a mystery as baffling as the *Price,* catching the attention of popular writers with it. The sturdy little steamer was built in 1907 in Scotland by A. McMillen & Sons. She was upbound from Sarnia for the Canadian shore of Lake Superior with a cargo of general freight including hay, canned goods and a deckload of heavy iron sewer and gas pipe. Supposedly when she passed up the St. Clair River and into Lake Huron, marine reporter Denny Lynn noted that he considered her deckload dangerous. "It didn't look too good at the time," he recalled. "I was afraid there would be trouble. I don't believe it is intended that boats of that description should be loaded in that manner."[5]

The heavy deckload clearly was dangerous, especially if stormy weather was encountered. Generally heavy material should be stowed lower in the ship and lighter goods higher. In simple terms, her loading was "upside down." Invariably this was caused by the planned unloading sequence. Material intended for the first stop was loaded last and last stop first. The problem was that putting heavy items like iron sewer pipe on top had several potential negative ramifications.

The *Regina* was slowly trying to work her way northward off Harbor Beach, Michigan, when last sighted by the steamer *Hawgood* whose captain remembered, "The seas were breaking over her." It was later surmised that she gave up butting into the waves and tried to turn back to Port Huron and shelter. She didn't make it. Off Port Sanilac, Michigan, the *Regina* was crushed by the waves and dove for the bottom. When divers finally discovered the wreck in 1986, roughly between Lexington and Port Sanilac on the Michigan side of the lake, they reported that her engine room telegraph was set at "All Stop," indicating that the captain had stopped the engines for some reason, perhaps in an effort to allow his crew to make a desperate effort to abandon ship in her lifeboats.

Largely intact, although upside down, she is in a shallow 75 to 80 feet of water. In 1913, there was speculation that she and the *Price* may have collided in the midst of the storm, causing the loss of both ships. After all, both were seen in close proximity and bodies from the *Regina* and *Price* were also found mixed together on the Canadian shore near Port Franks, 30 miles north of Sarnia. The collision theory was further fueled by the discovery that some of the *Regina* crew were wearing *Price* life jackets. The only explanation seemed to be that the *Price* crew hurriedly passed jackets to the *Regina* men in the confusion of the collision.

The sordid truth came out when four men saw local farmers and Port Franks residents hauling flotsam away from the beach. The men stopped the thieves, ordering them to return their plunder to the beach. But this was only the tip of the treasure hunting frenzy. Later investigation revealed local ghouls were busy plundering the dead of money and other valuables. Two of the bodies in the *Regina*'s lifeboat were found with their pockets turned out as were those on other bodies, a clear indication of robbing the dead. The loss of such personal articles doubtless made identification of the men more difficult. Perhaps the ghouls just viewed it all as gifts from the storm gods of the lake.

It was also rumored by some folks that a money belt containing $300 was missing from one of the sailors, but facts were few to verify the claim. Although Canadian officials started a patrol to find and protect the bodies as well as other wreckage, the locals had already done much harm. A government threat that the guilty parties would be arrested and charges could result with up to three years in prison if pilfered items were not returned did result in many items mysteriously returning to the beach.

The local Thedford undertaker was overwhelmed by the bodies, and at least 11 were laid out in a furniture store. Indoor space of any kind was at a premium. It was certainly a grisly display of human tragedy among the sales display of tables, chairs, sofas, beds and lamps. Having run out of blankets to drape the bodies, some had to be covered in old newspapers.

The freighter *Isaac M. Scott*, with Captain A. McArthur, a sister ship to the *Price*, was upbound on Huron for Milwaukee when the crashing seas pounded the steamer under with the loss of all 28 hands. The wreckage remained undiscovered until 1976, when it was located upside down in 200 feet of water, 7 miles northeast of Thunder Bay Island off Alpena, Michigan. Previously it was thought that she perished closer to the Canadian shore. Carrying coal, she evidently capsized after being blown into the deep and deadly wave trough. She was built in 1909 by the American Ship Building Company in Lorain.

The big steamer *Howard M. Hanna Jr.*, Captain William Hagan, was bound from Lorain to Fort William, Lake Superior with coal on her last trip of the season when the screaming wind and snarling seas slowly battered her apart. By 3 p.m. on the 9th she was off Pointe aux Barques, Michigan, and barely making headway. When 6:30 p.m. rolled around, the starboard oiler's door was smashed in and two engine room doors wrenched off. The engine room crew below was struggling through knee-deep ice water, and it was getting deeper. An hour later the cook's room and dining room were literally swept away, woodwork smashed from the walls and sent crashing down the companionway to the engine room, plus tables, chairs, pots and pans. After a particularly powerful wave slammed into her, cook Sadie Black also went tumbling down the companionway into the engine room as if on an amusement park water slide. Sadie wasn't a big lady, perhaps 100 pounds soaking wet, which she certainly was now, but she picked herself up and climbed right back to her duty station in the galley. No mere storm was going to keep her from her work!

Not long after that, the wheelhouse doors and windows ripped away, torn off by the pounding seas. The next wave knocked off the roof, sent flying into the stormy black night by the screaming wind. Many of the crew found shelter from the horrors of the storm in the steel lower deck cabins. Part of the stern cabin was battered into the lake and the stack disappeared into the storm, too.

By 10 p.m., the *Hanna* bridge crew caught a gleam of Port Austin Light and knew they were dangerously close to the deadly reefs. With a boat disintegrating under them, they had little choice but to drop the anchors, hold her off the reefs and just try to survive the deadly maelstrom. Considering the horrible conditions, it was a miracle that they were able to release the anchors at all, but they had virtually no effect, failing to hook into the bottom or perhaps just bouncing uselessly over the flat rock below.

It wasn't long before the big steamer was blown sideways onto Port Austin Reef, her steel hull howling in protest as it scraped over the unforgiving rock. She soon took on a starboard list and broke in two. Crashing waves began to knock off her hatch covers, opening the hull to quick flooding. The forward-end men were trapped and remainder of the 25 crew stuck aft. All were bound to the boat, since one of her two lifeboats and a single life raft had long been swept away. The water was far too wild to try to reach shore in the remaining boat.

Meanwhile, intrepid cook Sadie Black, despite a flooded galley, managed to get a fire going in the galley and soon provided the men aft with hot coffee and after a bit longer such hot food as she could rustle up from what supplies the waves hadn't spoiled or washed away. When the storm moderated on the following day, the mate was able make his way forward to the stranded front-end men with hot food, too.

The wreck was spotted by the lookout at the Port Austin Life-Saving Service station at 8:30 a.m. on the 10th through a rift in the snow squalls. She was 3 miles northwest of the station and a mile and a half off shore. Life-Saving Service Keeper John Frahm and his Life-Savers were in no position to render immediate help. Their boathouse containing both a big motor lifeboat and smaller surfboat was completely destroyed, just a pile of lumber collapsed over the boats and marine railway.

Surfman No. 1 Thomas Deegan telephoned the stations at Harbor Beach and Huron City, but both were already fully committed to their own wrecks and unable to help. With little choice, Frahm's men were forced to use an old surfboat stored behind the station. Although storm-damaged, she was the best bet for rescue. After dragging it down the beach to a point opposite the wreck, they launched into the still breaking seas and pulled for the beleaguered steamer. But the boat couldn't hold together in the tumbling waves, and the Life-Savers were forced to return to the beach after making barely half a mile. With no other option, they went to work on the pile of rubble that had been their boathouse. Eventually they managed to drag the badly damaged surfboat clear and after spending the night repairing her as best they could, given the situation, launched again the next morning into a somewhat calmer lake. On the way out they nearly sank, having to continually bail her out. Eventually they recovered all the *Hanna* crew except for six who came ashore in the steamer's last remaining lifeboat.[6]

Once they returned to shore they were greeted by townsfolk with pails of hot coffee. Later, rescuers and rescued were treated to a hearty dinner at a local hotel. Most charitably, the battered and leaky surfboat was returned to the station on a horse-drawn sleigh.[7]

Diminutive cook Sadie Black's efforts braving freezing waist-deep water in the galley to provide food to her trapped crew so impressed her crew that when finally rescued, they voted her a special cash purse in recognition of her valiant efforts.

The small steamer *Matoa,* bound from Toledo to Hancock on Lake Superior with coal, also died in the great storm. Just after midnight on the 9th, she was hammered onto Pointe aux Barques Reef about a mile and three-quarters east of the Life-Saving Service Station and roughly the same distance offshore. Despite the unholy howls of the wind, the lookout in the tower heard the wailing blasts of the ship's horn and answered with a red Coston flare, but in the hurricane conditions the Life-Savers were helpless to immediately go to the rescue. Waves were literally washing through the boathouse and the doors were already pounded off. The marine launchway as well as breakwater were washed away and the boathouse with the big motor lifeboat destroyed by the banshee-spawned storm. The men were helpless to assist anyone.

After frantic work, the crew was able to pull a semi-intact surfboat from the wreckage on the 11th and make their way out to the wreck that morning. The lake was still nasty and constant bailing was needed. They discovered that the *Matoa*'s crew of 20 were all safe, but after the sailors took a good look at the nearly wrecked surfboat, they decided they would stick with their steamer instead of taking a chance on the battered craft. The trip wasn't wasted, though, as the Life-Savers took back a message asking for a salvage tug.

On the morning of the 12th, the big tug *Favorite* arrived and started lightering coal, working until the 14th when building seas forced her off the wreck. She took the crew with her, leaving the *Matoa* to die on the reef, a reported loss of $123,000.[8]

Just up the coast the big casino at Harbor Beach was demolished by the storm, as were resort bowling alleys, boathouses, docks and pool halls. At the height of the storm at 11 p.m. on November 9, the big 6,598-ton steamer *D.O. Mills* ran hard up on the north reef about a half-mile offshore. She wasn't spotted until dawn on the 10th when the heavy snow squalls cleared. Unsure of her true condition, the Life-Savers ran out in their 34-foot motor lifeboat, but apparently no one was aboard. Since no one responded to their calls, they assumed the sailors were all huddled below, but the steamer appeared still sound.

During the night of the 10th, with moderating conditions, the *Mills* pumped herself out and neatly backed off the reef, helped by the heavy swells. It seems that the captain realized he was going onto the reef. So once up, he flooded his tanks, forcing his ship deeper into the water and solidly on the bottom. Luckily she was light (without cargo), making the escape easier than it would be on a fully laden ship. Legendary Life-Saving Keeper Ferris paid the captain high tribute for his fine seamanship. After her escapade, she went straight to the repair yard for $62,000 of work.

Other steamers found the beach, too. Captain A.C. May of the 532-foot *Henry A. Hawgood* was upbound light and getting the stuffings kicked out him. Until 1911, the steamer was part of the same company as the *Henry B. Smith*. Being such a snorter was bad enough, but without cargo to help him ride better was insane. He had seen the *Regina* battling past him, with the waves breaking clear over her deck and the same for the *Charles Price*. It likely sent a shiver down his spine. His wheelsman watched them, too, and 18-year-old Edward Kanaby didn't like what he saw either. It wasn't long before Kanaby could do something about it. When breakers suddenly appeared out of the blizzard dead ahead, Captain May ordered to turn seaward. Kanaby glanced at the terrible waves and instead turned hard for the sandy beach. Within minutes the big steamer rumbled aground. She wasn't going anywhere soon; mostly she wasn't going back out into the storm. When the blizzard cleared some, Kanaby noted that he went up directly in front of the Lake Huron Hotel at Lake Huron beach, near the Fort Gratiot Light.

Captain May eventually reported that his bow was out several feet and pointing directly toward the hotel. When the storm finally blew itself out, folks thought they could surely just walk out to the steamer. Salvage tugs would eventually pull her free.[9]

Another Hawgood steamer, the 414-foot *J.M. Jenks,* ended up ashore north of Midland on Georgian Bay.

The 2,300-ton British steamer *Arcadian* bound from Kingston, Lake Ontario, to Fort William on Lake Superior with $150,000 worth of cement and general freight was blown high on a reef off Sulphur Island, near Lake Huron's Thunder Bay. Although she was driven up on the 8th, the blinding snow prevented anyone from seeing her until the afternoon of the 10th, when word of her was finally carried to the Life-Saving Station 10 miles distant. The message was deceptively optimistic, saying although she was up on the reef, weather was moderating and the Life-Savers wouldn't be needed.

When the lake kicked up again the following day, however, the captain called for the Life-Savers to come out and stand by. It turns out that they were indeed needed. Legendary Keeper John Persons and his crew ran out in their 34-foot motor lifeboat and worked for several days helping wreckers save ship and cargo. Much of the effort involved shoveling cement into the lake, leaving their hands blistered and bleeding. For a surfman's hands, used to hours of rowing and boat work, to be bloodied in such effort speaks volumes to the challenge of this heavy work.

The crew returned to the station on the 17th and *Arcadian* floated off two days later. She was towed to Alpena for repair but suffered a loss of half the cargo and vessel value, a horrendous financial beating.[10]

While so many sailors perished, others survived by the slimmest of threads. When the beaches of eastern Lake Huron were piling up with the dead from the *Regina* and *Price,* not far away the battered steamer *Northern Queen* was hard on an offshore bar, driven up on Sunday night. Watchers from the safety of the beach thought her 22 crewmen were surely dead men walking, since the ship was broken aft and slowly coming apart in the thundering waves. Every time a sea smashed into the ship, they could see her shudder with the impact. Unfortunately there was no Canadian version of the U.S. Life-Saving Service standing ready to battle out to them. Even worse, the nearest town was Port Franks and all communication wires were down, cutting her off from the world and making calls for outside help impossible. The men on the beleaguered steamer had to work out a scheme for their own salvation. Those ashore could only pray that the weather broke before the ship did.

Lake Huron's Canadian shore was littered with lost sailors.

Around noon the men on the steamer carefully lowered one of their lifeboats into the seething water.[11] By a miracle it survived being battered against the hull and one by one 10 of the men leaped into the wildly jumping boat. The crew took up oars and rowed for the beach. Though they showed none of the skill or dexterity of a Life-Saving crew, they slowly breasted the waves crawling for the shore. As the lifeboat crested the final breaker, local men pushed out into the surf, grabbed the gunwales and hauled it up to the beach. All 10 men survived.

Incredibly, two of the crewmen, wet and shaking with cold, volunteered to take the boat back to the steamer to rescue their companions! The quality of courage can never truly be measured until it is most direly needed. In this instance, looking deep into the chasm of the breaking seas, it was a test to measure every man against. The two men started well enough, rowing hard and cresting the tumbling seas until some distance out a monster wave tossed the boat over, spilling them into the lake. Both started swimming back for the beach. One was slightly ahead of the other when he glanced back at

The citizens of Goderich interned the remains of unidentified sailors under a single monument.

his companion. Seeing him falter in distress, he quickly swam back and grabbed him. Together they made the long struggle for shore. As with the lifeboat, as soon as they reached safe water, others rushed from the beach to drag them to safety.

After seeing the failure of their rescue, the men on the steamer launched a second lifeboat, and nine of them reached shore without harm. When the weather finally moderated, Captain Crawford, First Mate William McDonald and the second mate, who stayed with him on the ship, came ashore in the last remaining lifeboat.

How the *Northern Queen* ended up on the beach speaks to the true power of the storm. Crew members later told a local newspaper reporter that the steamer passed Port Huron upbound at 9 a.m. Sunday, November 9. Lake Huron was blowing hard and storm flags were flying, but foul weather was just part of fall on the lakes, so the steamer plowed on into the seas. The farther north she ran the worse the storm became until about 40 miles up when she could no longer make headway against the thundering seas. Captain Crawford considered whether he should try to turn around to head back for Port Huron when a monster wave slammed into the steamer, turning it 180 degrees! With the decision made for him, he made his way south. About 4:30 a.m. the next day, she was a mile off Fort Gratiot Lighthouse.

Now things became confusing very quickly. They could see the lights of a steamer ahead of them but in the fury of the storm couldn't determine if she was under way, drifting or aground.[12] At this point a watchman heard signals from the lighthouse fog horn, which they interpreted as a warning rather that the normal sound sequence. Believing the signals meant "danger ahead," the captain and mate swung the *Northern Queen* around and again took a northerly course. Again, the full fury of wind and wave smashed into her as she strained to butt her way into the seas. After running 30 miles, she was stopped dead by the battering seas. Afraid to risk another turn south, Captain Crawford dropped anchor, doubtless running out every foot of chain he had. Given the beating from the storm, he wasn't certain where he was but thought he could hold position until the storm blew itself out. In reality he was about 8 miles off Port Franks, Ontario. As blast after blast struck the steamer, her anchors bounced along the bottom and the *Northern Queen* drove onto the beach, striking about 7 p.m. November 10, going bow up into shore.[13]

The storm winds forced the Port Huron lightship marking the entrance to the St. Clair River far off her position. In the aftermath of the storm, famous salvor Tom Reid located her and, knowing her importance to shipping, offered to tow her back for a small fee. The lightship captain refused, stating that he could only agree after getting permission from district headquarters in Chicago.[14] With the current state of downed telegraph lines that, of course, wasn't going to be anytime soon. Meanwhile the captain of the downbound 532-foot steamer *Matthew Andrews*, storm battered but not broken, was looking for the lightship to find the channel. Without it to mark the way, he did his best, but ran up on Corsica Shoal instead.

Chapter 5

Superior Screamed

Ships on Lake Superior faced their own brand of hell and, like those in other lakes, some survived while others perished. At the height of the blow more than 50 ships anchored for shelter between the Sault Ste. Marie and Whitefish Point. Among the fleet was the famous Canadian Pacific Railroad steamer *Alberta*, sister ship to the *Algoma*, which wrecked at Isle Royale with the loss of roughly 40 passengers and crew in another November storm 28 years earlier. Even a protected anchorage wasn't foolproof. Several of the steamers were so buffeted by wind and wave, they snapped their heavy anchor chains. One lost both.

The 249-foot Canadian freighter *Leafield*, under Captain Charles Baker and owned by the Algoma Central Steamship Line with a heavy cargo of steel rail, was reportedly smashed against tiny Angus Island, 14 miles southeast of Thunder Bay, Ontario, in the western end of the lake.[1] Built as a "three island freighter" in 1892 in Scotland for ocean trading, she was considered extremely seaworthy. Regardless, her entire crew of 18 men perished, swallowed forever by Lake Superior's frigid waters. It was speculated that she slipped off the reef in the fury of the storm, disappearing in the deep water. At least a dozen of her crew listed Collingwood, Ontario, at the foot of Georgian Bay as home. Collingwood's maritime traditions run deep. It was a terminus for rail-to-water shipping to old Fort William/Port Arthur on Lake Superior and Chicago, as well as shipbuilding, including the first steel vessel built in Canada. Many fine sailors came out of Collingwood.

The *Leafield* was lost with all hands. She is still among Superior's "went missing" fleet. MARITIME MUSEUM

The *Leafield* could have been considered a doomed ship even before the storm, both her sister ships lost in the same area earlier. In November 1905, the *Monkshaven* wrecked near Angus Island, and the following year the *Theano* sank near Trowbridge Island.[2] The previous year, the *Leafield* went up on the rocks of Beausoleil Island in Georgian Bay with extensive hull damage, repaired by the next season.

An alternative *Leafield* theory postulates that during the height of the storm, locals mistook the wreckage of the *Monkshaven,* still on Angus Island, for the *Leafield.* Thus in reality the *Leafield* could be east of Angus Island in deep water or, for that matter, in virtually any location on the lake. There is no record of any wreckage field to point to even a general area of loss.

Just to make it more confusing, when Captain Baird of the steamer *Hamonic* arrived in Fort William, he claimed that he saw the end of the *Leafield*, stating she crested a huge wave and suddenly lurched forward, diving for the bottom. None of the crew had a chance to put on a life preserver. He gave no location for the sinking.[3]

A lesser tragedy was unfolding in the eastern lake. The 377-foot steel steamer *William Nottingham* was slowly working her way into shelter in Whitefish Bay on November 11 when she went hard up on a reef between Ile Parisienne and South Sandy islands.[4] For two days she pounded hard in the grip of the storm, finally buckling

There is some thought the wreckage of the *Monkshaven*, still on Pie Island from the infamous November 1905 storm, was mistaken for that of the *Leafield*.
K.E. THRO COLLECTION

amidships.⁵ Both her food and fuel ran out. Without the heat from her boilers, the men would freeze to death. The fuel problem was partially solved by burning her wood cabin trim and furniture and finally part of her wheat cargo, firemen throwing great shovels of it into the boiler fires. Likely they had to break a hatch open and carry the grain down to the fireroom load by load. It must have been a grueling process, but desperate men will do desperate things. Food was urgently needed, too.

Finally her yawl boat was launched with three volunteers: a wheelsman, oiler and deckhand. With luck they could reach the beach and send for help. The boat barely dropped the blocks before it was dashed by the waves against the high steel side of the hull, overturning and drowning all three men. Eventually help did reach the *Nottingham*, and the crew was saved. Salvagers later released the ship, but repair costs were very high. She was built by the Buffalo Union Dry Dock Company in 1902.⁶

Captain Noble and the steamer *Cornell* had an especially desperate experience. She rounded Whitefish Point upbound at 6:30 p.m. on Friday, November 7. The wind blew light southeasterly. At midnight a heavy northwest sea began pounding into her. The motion of the ship was soon severe enough that the wheel was frequently spun out of the water, necessitating an engineer to stand by and to throttle back to prevent the machinery from self-destructing.

At 2 a.m., the wind shifted north to gale force with blinding snow, and the boat soon picked up a heavy coating of ice. Captain Noble estimated that she was 89 miles above Whitefish Point. At this point the mate, who was on duty in the pilothouse, became severely ill, whether from the violent motion of the ship or other cause is unknown. To ease getting him back to his cabin Captain Noble turned the *Cornell* before the wind. Once the mate was safely below, the captain was unable to come back to his course. Even at full power, he couldn't muscle her around against wind and wave.

Trapped broadside to the seas, she was driving fast to the deadly lee shore. The *Cornell* was rolling so severely that the crew couldn't operate her sounding machine.[7] Even copious amounts of oil pumped from her hawse holes to form a slick to reduce the seas was ineffective. Had she not been empty of cargo, it is worth considering that she could have shifted cargo and capsized, adding her to the growing list of dead ships.

She lay in the trough until 3:30 a.m. Saturday. When it was apparent that the beset steamer was fast approaching the beach, Captain Noble dropped an anchor with 50 fathoms of chain. It didn't even slow her down! When he could clearly see the trees, he dropped his second anchor with all 90 fathoms of chain. By using the anchors as a pivot point and driving his engine full ahead ("Give me all you have, Scotty!"), Captain Noble was able to force his bow around, but not before a hand lead showed a mere 8 fathoms under his keel.

The *Cornell* remained in her precarious position until 7:20 a.m. Sunday with her engine running constantly at full speed ("She can't take it, Captain!"). She was only a mile off the beach and 5 miles or so from the Deer Park Life-Saving Station. Should an anchor drag or chain break, she was a certain wreck.

At 2:30 p.m. on Sunday, the wind dropped enough for Captain Noble to haul his anchors and take a northeasterly course off the beach. The steamer didn't escape without damage. The terrific strain on the anchors caused a cat's paw and chock to carry away and damaged the wildcat, forcing the captain to use the compressor to hold the anchors in place.[8]

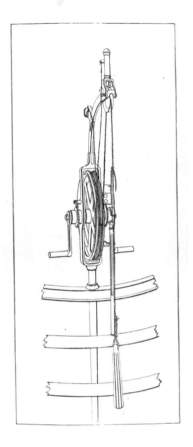

Great Lakes freighters during this period were equipped with "sounding machines" to determine water depth. The alternative was a "hand lead."
U.S. PATENT OFFICE

At 10 p.m. Sunday, the *Cornell* was somewhere southeast of Caribou Island when a howling northeast gale slammed into her. Half an hour later, she was deep in the trough again and rolling her guts out. Dropping an anchor again allowed Captain Noble to force his way before the wind.

At 6 a.m., a gigantic wave broke over the stern, hammering off the cabin overhang, smashing all of her doors and windows, and flooding both dining rooms and all cabins save the chief engineer's. The woodwork and fixtures in the dining rooms were reduced to kindling. Again oil was pumped out of the hawse pipes and even thrown overboard by the bucketful. It had little effect. The waves were running even larger than the behemoths pummeling the *Cornell* on Saturday. The steamer continued to be driven southerly by the hurricane blasts.

By 3 p.m. Monday, the crew caught sight of a beach to the south through a gap in the blinding snow. Captain

Noble immediately dropped an anchor with a full 90 fathom run of chain in a desperate effort to bring her head around. When the first anchor failed to do the job, the second one went down. Both held long enough to pull her into the sea with full engine power. Minutes later the wildcat broke, sending the second anchor and chain rattling off forever into the depths. Luckily, by keeping the engine full ahead and masterfully using her rudder, Captain Noble was able to keep the *Cornell* heading into the huge seas.

By this time Captain Noble estimated that he was only 2 to 3 miles off the beach, somewhere between the Two-Hearted River and Crisp's Point. The hand lead showed only 10 fathoms of water.

Around 5:30 p.m. Monday the wind moderated and Captain Noble hove his remaining anchor but was soon pushed back into the trough and again started for the beach. Down rumbled his only anchor again, and again he was able to swing her back out of the trough with his engine.

Finally at 10:30 p.m. the moderating seas allowed Captain Noble to drive the *Cornell* off the deadly shore. The battered steamer and weary crew reached the Soo at 7 a.m. Tuesday.[9] They escaped a deadly dance with death on Lake Superior.

The Northern Navigation Company (a division of Canada Steamship Lines) big passenger steamer *Huronic* went ashore at Whitefish Point. With visibility near zero in the blinding snow, her captain was trying to duck in behind the point for shelter from the smashing northwest seas when he went up. Luckily the bottom was sandy and she wasn't greatly damaged. The crew and passengers remained safe aboard until tugs arrived to haul her free after two days aground. Doubtless passengers had a great tale to tell of their shipwreck adventure during the Great Storm.

Deeper into Whitefish Bay, the big steamers *J.T. Hutchinson* and *Fred G. Hartwell* found the rocks at Point Iroquois. Captain H.J. Yaques and the *Hutchinson* made a desperate run down the lake from Isle Royale on Sunday,

The Northern Navigation Company steamer *Huronic* was driven ashore at Whitefish Point.
MARINE HISTORICAL COLLECTION

all the while hammered by the storm. He tried to hide behind the lee of Caribou Island, but the shifting wind around the island defeated him. When he finally turned Whitefish Point, he thought he was safe, but in the blizzard and pounding storm, he ended up on the rocks at Point Iroquois. It wasn't long before the *Hartwell* went up just to his east.

A short time later Captain Warren C. Jones of the steamer *Sylvania* decided that it was time to leave his safe Whitefish Point anchorage and head out, upbound. The wind had been slowly dropping during the afternoon so at 5 p.m. he hauled anchor and soon turned the point, bound up, entering the same "sucker hole" that Captain Owen did with the *Smith*. Within an hour he was smashed by the storm. The wind literally turned the *Sylvania* 180 degrees and was driving her bow first for the beach. He tried to stop by putting her into full reverse. It did no good, only driving her stern into the mountainous waves. In desperation, he dropped his anchor with 35 fathoms of chain in the hope it would grab the bottom and swing his bow around into the sea, halting his inexorable drive for the shore. It was a dangerous act. If the anchor caught there was the very real chance as the ship swung around and came parallel to the waves it would be caught in the trough long enough to capsize. The maneuver worked. The *Sylvania* came around, the anchor held and she was kept off the beach.

Captain T.J. Cullen of the steamer *William Edenborn* hung on his Whitefish Bay anchor a bit longer, deciding to depart on Monday. After turning the point west, he couldn't make any headway against the monster seas and hellacious wind, so he anchored. After waiting until things calmed a bit, he tried again, and again he couldn't make headway. So again the chain rattled down into the dark water. It took him several tries before he was finally able to finish his trip, and a rough one it was.

Although the old wood propeller *Major* survived the storm, it was a near thing. The 283-foot freighter was built by F. Wheeler in West Bay City, Michigan, in 1889 and upbound with coal. She was the largest wood vessel left on the lakes. Off Whitefish Point, the northwest blast of wind forced her into the wave trough. With her cargo shifted, half filled with water and with her upper works swept away, the crew decided it was time to leave her. A crew member later claimed, "She was rapidly going to pieces when she was abandoned. The old tub was crumbling like so much chalk. I never imagined a boat could go to pieces in such a short time."[10]

Luckily, the steamer *A.M. Byers* spotted her distress signals and with a remarkable piece of expert ship handling managed to rescue her captain and his 18-man crew. Captain A. Craigee was able to deftly nudge the bow of his 525-foot steamer against the bow of the *Major* long enough to allow her crew to leap to safety, including the ship's dog. The *Major* was abandoned as a derelict, but surprised everyone by surviving the storm. Salvaged, she was sold to a Canadian fleet, eventually becoming a floating drydock.

When the captain of a Hines Lumber Company steamer staggered into Portage Lake, he told everyone, "It was the worst storm I have ever experienced. ... We had just passed the Huron Islands and were approaching Point Abbaye when the blow struck. It was the most peculiar storm I have ever seen. The wind, snow and waves came at the same time, and if we were 25 miles out, I'm afraid it would have been a toss of a coin whether we could have weathered the blow. At times the rail was beneath water and we pitched with unusual violence. Large boxes of coal carried on deck were tossed around like so many chips. Fortunately for us the entry was close and after a stormy passage we passed inside the breakwater. Not until then did we feel safe."[11]

In a similar tale many folks gave the old wooden steamer *Simon Langell* and her two consorts up for lost before they miraculously staggered through the Duluth canal.

The master of the Pittsburgh Steamship Company steamer *Alexander McDougall* reported very difficult conditions on Lake Superior. Captain F.D. Selee had frightening problems securing his wooden hatch covers. By design they were held in place (supposedly tightly) by wood wedges, but the wedges washed away in boarding seas, leaving the covers adrift.

The *McDougall* was downbound from the Superior, Wisconsin, docks on November 9 and running under the north shore to shelter from the shattering north winds and seas. Worried about his hatches staying secure, Captain Selee lay to under Otter Head to check and refasten where needed. He discovered many of the wedges gone, washed overboard by the boarding seas. The crew tightened the hatches as best they could with what spare wedges were available, but it was strictly a stopgap at best. Resuming his run to the Soo, he noticed that the hatches were continuing to loosen.

Blinded by the snow, he was running strictly by compass and not certain of his position, but his reckoning showed that he was near to Whitefish Point. In his words, "I had the mate on the end of the bridge with deep sea lead going as our sounding machine was frozen up in 2 feet of ice and could not use it. I sent the second mate and one wheelsman down in the forepeak to listen for the submarine bell at Whitefish.[12] I had the boatswain and other wheelsman on the lookout and at 10:05 (a.m.) the second mate reported he could hear the bell off Whitefish and at 10:25 we had it abreast. We came around Whitefish from the sound of that bell from the forepeak. We could not see Whitefish." When she eventually reached Sault Ste. Marie, half of the wooden hatch wedges were missing, driven out by the deck-borne waves. In his report to the company, he stressed the criticality of having lateral strongbacks across all hatch covers with tarpaulins on top.[13]

The big Cleveland Cliffs vessel *William G. Mather* also made the downbound run on the north route. In contrast to the *McDougall,* her trip was comparatively uneventful. I stress *comparatively*! Captain F.A. West and the *Mather* hauled into Ashland, Wisconsin, Friday morning, November 7, after an easy run down from Superior, Wisconsin. Based on the weather forecast and his low barometer (28.80), the captain was expecting a much rougher trip to Ashland than it turned out to be. He wasted no time in port; loading chutes started dumping ore into her at 7 a.m. By 10 a.m., it was raining hard, but loading continued until noon. After the midday meal, the wind and rain increased to the point that the ore dock crews refused to work. After the weather somewhat moderated in the afternoon, they returned to work, finishing the job at 6 p.m.

Meanwhile the weather bureau advised the dock that storm warnings were posted as of 10 a.m., storm winds starting southwest and shifting to the northwest. When the *Mather* backed away from the dock at 7 p.m., the rain was coming down hard and wind screaming north. Just after clearing the dock and starting ahead for her downbound run, she was battered by a blizzard of snow and gale force winds. Discretion being the better part of valor, Captain West dropped both anchors and remained safe in the harbor.

When it stopped snowing shortly after midnight, the sky cleared and stars were visible. The wind dropped off, too. Thinking that the storm was over, the captain hove anchors at 1 a.m. on the 8th and headed for the Soo. The glass had bumped up, too, settling on 29.20. Even experienced captains make mistakes in reading the weather.

On clearing Michigan Island at 4:19 a.m., the steamer was smacked hard by a rising northwest sea and wind.

As soon as he was able, Captain West swung north by east, holding the course until reaching the calm water along the north shore of Minnesota later in the day. The slog north had been tough. From 6 a.m. until 10 a.m., all the while bucking into the strong seas, she managed to make only 17 miles. Captain West noted that the wind was "light," however, only 40 mph! But the seas were monsters.

Captain West later stated that he wasn't able to go ahead fast enough. Several times he was afraid he would lose his steerage way and broach. If he did, a cargo shift and capsize was near certain. He noted, "The weather was getting colder as we were icing up very bad; our wire life line had got to be about the size of a hawser and sagged down almost to the deck. It was a wonder to me it did not break." The iced-over decks prevented the forward crew from going aft for chow, missing both breakfast and dinner.[14]

Captain West used his seaman's instinct to good advantage later, relating, "We passed Rock of Ages Light at 5:15 p.m. and the weather again looked good, almost tempting me to go to the southward of Isle Royale, but the barometer was not acting right – it was still hanging at 29.20, the same as when we left Ashland, with the wind from the north and still blowing hard. So I decided to continue down the north shore where we had comparatively smooth water."

After passing Battle Island at 4:40 a.m. on November 9, he swung southeast to pass the west side of Michipicoten Island, but a rising sea and heavy north-northeast wind forced him to the east-southeast between the island and Otter Head. Blinding snow again blotted out everything, causing complete reliance on dead reckoning navigation. Although rolling hard, the *Mather* was making good time.

Passing the east light on Michipicoten at 2 p.m., the weather looked reasonably good. The wind lulled and the sun presented a bright blue sky. By all indications the improving weather meant an easy run to Whitefish Point. Two hours later the weather dragon struck again, the sleeping storm roaring awake with greater intensity than anything previously faced.

At 9:12 p.m., the pilothouse crew picked up Whitefish Point Light through a hole in the snow. Conditions were truly horrible, with blinding snow, immense waves and blasting wind. The only way Captain West could hold his course past Whitefish and keep from falling into the trough was to hold the rudder nearly hard-a-port.

Captain West later reported, "The snow by this time was a blizzard, you could not look into it and the wind was a continuous roar. We could not hear our own whistle forward. The after part of our weather cloth was blown to pieces. The forward part had about four inches of ice on it or that would have gone, too."

Once she finally cleared Whitefish at 11:20 p.m., Captain West "… put (his) wheel hard-a-starboard and came up head to the wind and let go of our port anchor and gave her all the chain in 20 fathoms of water, but she walked away with it. We then gave her the starboard anchor and at 11:50 p.m. they got a hold, but we dragged quite a distance.

"It continued to snow and blow without any apparent letup until 9 a.m. Monday morning, the 10th. It cleared up a little at that time and we found we had dragged down into a fleet of steamers at anchor. The *M.A. Hanna* was about a quarter of a mile to the northward of us, the *Peter A.B. Widener* about three boat lengths under our stern and the *Princeton* was on our port quarter, all together about 15 steamers.

"It began to clear by noon. We hove up our anchor at 1 p.m. November 10. It was still snowing some, but the sky was clearing and the wind had now gotten down to an ordinary gale. We arrived at the canal at 3 p.m. after passing through the largest fleet of wind-bound steamers I think I ever saw at one time. They were anchored above Big Point with both anchors down and they almost completely blocked the channel. There was also a fleet in the canal, mostly headed down – steamers that had lost both anchors and had to make the canal."[15]

When the steamer *Winona* put into Marquette's Presque Isle Harbor, the winds were so strong that her captain decided not to come up the dock but instead just put her fast on a sandbar, and flooded down his tanks to make certain she stayed hard on the bottom.[16]

Normally Shot Point, about 8 miles east of the city, is easily visible to folks in the harbor. But when the blizzard dropped a curtain of white on everything, frantic rumors flew that a big laker was aground on the point. Only when the blizzard let up was the rumor proved false.

Other ships and crews may have survived the terrible storm, but there was no redemption for the *Henry B. Smith* and her crew. When she pulled away from the dock in Marquette, she sailed into deadly legend.

Chapter 6

Fate Will Choose

Carnage reigned throughout the Great Lakes – ships foundering, lifeless crew drifting on the beach frozen in grotesque shapes, ships driven ashore by hurricane blasts, some sliding up on easy sand bottoms, others finding steel-killing rock. The very fortunate ones made safe harbor, entering battered and damaged, sheathed in thick ice.

On Lake Superior one ship was supremely lucky and one equally abandoned by the gods. Histories of the 1913 storm traditionally treat their stories separately, just two ships meeting their own private disaster. But there are threads that tie them together in a fashion, the strongest of which is "what might have been. ..."

This chilling dance of circumstance began on Friday, November 7, 11:45 p.m. when the 451-foot, 4,422-ton steamer *L.C. Waldo* departed Two Harbors, Minnesota, just after dawn with iron ore for Cleveland. The lake was churned by a stiff so'wester, giving the steamer good roll.

The *Waldo,* owned by the Roby Transportation Company, was built in 1896 by the F.W. Wheeler Company of Bay City, Michigan, and named for the company manager. She was considered a fine-looking vessel when she came out of the yard. As typical of the era, she had a turret-style pilothouse with an open bridge above. By 1913, a wooden upper pilothouse, often called a "wheelhouse" enclosing the old open bridge, was added. Enclosed pilothouses were becoming commonplace since they offered far more protection to the crews in foul weather.

The *L.C. Waldo* often loaded ore in Marquette.

The *Henry B. Smith* arrived in Marquette the same day, late on Thursday night. It was a rough trip up Superior as the original southwest gale swung strong northwest. Captain Owen was anxious to load and be on his way back to Cleveland, a run of nearly 600 miles. Given a quick turnaround, he could even beat the *Waldo* to the Sault Ste. Marie.

The *Waldo* was having her own problems, and they were serious indeed. The deeper into the lake she went, the worse the storm became, but the *Waldo* slowly struggled on, working her way through the ravages of wind and wave as best she could. About midnight on Friday, when she was still west of Keweenaw Point (a rocky projection often called "Old Treacherous" by sailors), a set of rogue seas boarded the steamer. These "fists of Neptune" wrenched off her wheelhouse, nearly tearing off the entire forecastle, seriously damaging her steering gear and knocking out her electric lighting system. The greatest loss was the compass and binnacle, going overboard with the wheelhouse.

Captain John W. Duddleson of Sault Ste. Marie, Michigan, First Mate Charles Keefer and Wheelsman Bernard Foley were nearly killed when the wheelhouse went overboard. The captain and mate escaped by diving down the companionway to the cabin below while the wheelsman held on to what was left of the house. Once the wave passed, the two men clambered back up through the wreckage and surveyed the damage, including the

The L.C. Waldo was downbound from Two Harbors when the storm smashed into her.

injured Foley. Captain Duddleson was nothing if not resourceful. On his orders a brave crewman dashed off into the blackness and grabbed a compass from a lifeboat. After lashing it off to a wood stool, illuminated by the yellow glow of a flickering oil lantern, Captain Duddleson and Second Mate Feeger used the emergency steering apparatus to try to keep the steamer on course.

It was a surrealistic scene: The snow blotted out all vision beyond the range of the dim lantern, the ship wildly pitched and rolled, the thundering of wind and sea mixed with the screech of another piece of *Waldo* being torn off by the storm. Unsure of his position in the howling gale and snowstorm, the captain planned to work his way between Gull Rock and Keweenaw Point. It was a narrow, rock-strewn cut, but offered the best chance to save his ship. Once clear of the passage, he would swing to starboard and find shelter behind the hook of the Keweenaw Peninsula. The seas around the point were hellish, striking the rockbound peninsula and offshore islands, ricocheting back to create a maelstrom of cross seas.

Captain Duddleson later told awe-struck listeners he could look back and see waves crashing over his stern cabin, burying all but the stack. There was no doubt that when he later claimed the storm "…was the worst he had ever experienced in his nearly 40 years of sailing," he meant every word. When his storm adventure finished, the 65-year-old master reputedly "swallowed the anchor" and took a shore job in the Soo. He claimed that he would never sail again.

Below in the engine room, the watch kept the boiler fires burning. With the extreme pitching and rolling of the steamer, just shoveling coal into the fireboxes was difficult. Regardless, the *Waldo*'s propeller continued to turn, giving the desperately beleaguered steamer a chance to live.

On the *Smith,* Captain Owen may have been anxious to load and go, but for the time being he was safely moored to the Duluth, South Shore and Atlantic ore dock in Marquette. Out on the open lake, ships and crews like the *Waldo* were dying. He was damned lucky and didn't know it.

Disaster struck the *Waldo* about 4 a.m. on Saturday, November 8, when she plowed dead onto Gull Rock Reef. The lethal projection of rock extends westward from Gull Island toward the tip of the Keweenaw. To keep his ship from sliding off the ledge into deep water and perhaps sinking, the captain ordered his engineer to "flood her down," filling her ballast tanks literally to lock her to the reef. The chief did the best he could, but in the howling storm not all tanks were flooded. Unfortunately, those that were did the job. Battered by the mammoth waves, the *Waldo* soon cracked in two amidships. Captain Duddleson, afraid that the stern would break off and sink in deep water, immediately ordered all aboard to the forward cabins. It was a dangerous run for the crew across the iced-over, wave-washed deck, but all arrived safely. The hasty evacuation, however, cut the crew off from the galley aft, as well as warm clothes left in their cabins. The steam pipes from the engine room fractured when the hull broke, leaving them without heat. The crew of 24, including two women, huddled in freezing despair,

The light at Gull Rock was already extinguished for the season.
WAYNE SAPULSKI COLLECTION

knowing the end was near. The only food they had were two one-gallon cans of stewed tomatoes and a can of peaches hastily grabbed by a crewman running through the galley while rushing forward.

The women, the steward's wife, Mrs. Arthur Rice, and her mother, Mrs. Mackie, were in the dining room aft when the *Waldo* drove into the deadly reef. Both reportedly became hysterical, refusing to leave the illusionary safety of the cabin to go forward with the men. Given their lack of sailing experience, how else could they react in the midst of such a terrifying situation? Even seasoned mariners sometimes panicked in an emergency. Finally four crewmen, including the steward, literally dragged them across 400 feet of utterly black ice-covered open deck to reach the forecastle.

Doubtless the men remembered the terrible fate of the crew of the big steel steamer *Mataafa* in the November 1905 storm. She struck bottom in tremendous seas while trying to make it through the Duluth entry. Driven by wind and wave, she ended up sideways to the shore and breaking in two. Heroic work by the Life-Savers rescued all of the crew trapped forward, but the nine caught aft froze to death. Was the *Mataafa* a precursor to their fate?

By Saturday morning, November 8, the *Smith* finally began to load ore, or at least tried to fill her cavernous

The big steel steamer *L.C. Waldo* hard on Gull Rock Reef.

holds. In fact loading was nearly impossible. Friday's balmy mid-50s temperatures had plummeted to the mid-20s. The storm picked up in power, too, with the sheltered harbor recording speeds of nearly 50 mph. It was certainly far worse on the open lake.

Regardless of the weather delays, the *Smith* could still make at least one more trip this season. The Marquette docks wouldn't close until November 28.

Given the wetness of earlier snow and cold temperatures, the ore was freezing in the dock pockets, and getting it to drop down the chutes and into the ship was nearly impossible. Ore also froze in the railcars. Regardless of the captain's protestations about the need to load his ship quickly, the dock master finally gave up, sending his loading crew home early. They would try again on Saturday when the weather promised to moderate. Captain Owen could only lament another lost day in port. Regardless, he reportedly optimistically wired the owners, "I will clear as soon as the ore is aboard. I am coming." Whether he actually did so or not is questionable and will be examined later.

The *Henry B. Smith* would have loaded much as this vessel did. Note the "dock wallopers" with the long poles to break up the ore jams.

Aboard the *Waldo*, the situation was rapidly descending into life and death. The same cold that froze the *Smith*'s ore was slowly killing the *Waldo* crew. Only the ingenuity of chief engineer Albert Lembke saved the crew from immediately freezing to death. Dragging the captain's heavy iron bathtub to the windlass room, he turned it upside down on the steel deck, leaving one end propped up. He had the crew knock the ends out of the emergency fire buckets. Fitting them together into a makeshift chimney, he ran it from the tub's drain out a dead light,[1] transforming the tub into an expedient stove. Cabin furniture was broken up and used as firewood. Since there wasn't enough room for all of the crew to stay next to the bathtub simultaneously, the captain divided them into groups to take turns exercising for warmth, gathering wood and huddling around the smoky tub. Captain Duddleson later said that one of the men refused to take a turn gathering wood, but after being excluded from a chance to get near the stove, he quickly changed his mind. Supposedly, when the steamer hit the rocks the impact overturned the captain's safe, spilling money all over the floor, but no one bothered to pick it up. Life was so uncertain, money lost its value.

The steamer *George Stephenson*, savior of the imperiled crew of the *L.C. Waldo*.

As the frigid hours passed, the *Waldo* became thickly coated in ice, resembling a grotesque ice sculpture. Ice also covered the doors and dead lights, trapping the desperate crew inside their frozen hell. Encased by the ice, freezing despite the makeshift stove and starving to death, the crew despaired, increasingly convinced of the utter hopelessness of their plight. No one even knew they were there. Surely they would perish. They were just dead men walking.

Even the lighthouse gods were working against the *Waldo*. Mere months earlier, Gull Rock Light was automated. While the light duly came on and off, no human keeper stood witness to the unfolding disaster or could possibly summon aid.

But unknown to the *Waldo* crew, they had been sighted. Late Saturday, November 8, Captain A.C. Mosher of the 407-foot Pittsburgh steamer *George Stephenson* arrived on the scene. The *Stephenson* was upbound and taking a terrific beating from the storm. Blinded by the snow, Captain Mosher navigated his way into Keweenaw Bay at 5 p.m., finding the 12-fathom line by sounding with the hand lead. He anchored for the night under the welcoming shelter of Keweenaw Point. On the morning of November 9, his men sighted an unknown steamer fast upon Gull Rock Reef. Minutes later a distress flag rattled up the stranger's pole. Captain Mosher promptly dipped his ensign in reply but saw no response.

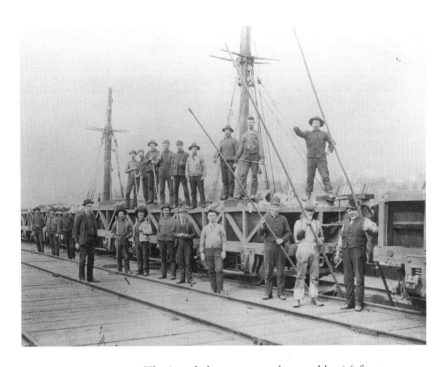

The Marquette dock wallopers were critical to the efficient loading of ore freighters.

The impaled steamer was battered by 16-foot waves, blasting into her stern and rolling up the weather deck to smash into the forecastle. Captain Mosher noted that her boats were still aboard. Clearly her crew was trapped. Hauling his anchor, he turned his ship westerly following the south shore of the peninsula.

The pounding of the relentless seas stripped the *Waldo* of anything on the weather deck that could be knocked off, sending a mass of flotsam into the wild lake. Reportedly 76 sections of wooden hatches, three "lifeboats" (most likely only yawls), pieces of her wooden deck cabin and numerous marked life belts washed ashore just west of Big Bay Point. The *Marquette Chronicle* reporter who reputedly visited the wreckage site described the belts as of the "old seaweed filled" variety, so waterlogged that each "weighed 200 pounds."[2]

Sunday, November 9, was no better loading weather for the *Smith*, but the dock wallopers in Marquette beat, hammered and prodded the frozen ore. With the strong

Eagle Harbor Life-Saving Service Station deep in winter's icy grip.
MICHIGAN TECHNOLOGICAL UNIVERSITY ARCHIVES

northwest winds and temperatures in the mid-20s, it was cold, miserable work for the dock workers. The men needed frequent breaks in the work shed, gathering about a glowing wood stove to briefly warm up and down a mug of hot Joe before again attacking the frozen ore.

Captain Mosher slowly brought the *Stephenson* toward shelter off Mendota. It was far calmer behind the bulk of the Keweenaw Peninsula, but it wasn't water he normally sailed, so caution was in order if his idea was to work. Bete Grise is about 13 miles west of Gull Rock.

He knew that the only hope for the crew on the stranded steamer was the U.S. Life-Saving Service Station at Eagle Harbor. Period charts were marked with station locations, so the sailors were constantly reminded of their position. Time and again the Life-Savers came to the aid of sailors, earning the surfmen great respect in the maritime community. Now the storm warriors were needed again. With a volunteer crew, the mate lowered the lifeboat, rowed ashore and landed at Mendota, where he hired a fisherman with a small motorboat to take him across Lac La Belle. He then took a horse and sleigh 8 frigid miles through the teeth of a blizzard to the small copper mining village of Delaware, where a little

Keeper Charles Tucker of Eagle Harbor.

KEWEENAW COUNTY HISTORICAL SOCIETY, MARITIME COMMITTEE

before noon Sunday, November 9, he telephoned the news to the lighthouse keeper at Eagle Harbor on the west side of the Keweenaw.[3] The Eagle Harbor Life-Saving Station on the other side of the harbor from the lighthouse only just became operational the year before, and a direct telephone line was not yet installed. The lightkeeper ran a prearranged white signal flag up his pole, which was immediately spotted by Surfman Chester Tucker on duty in the Life-Saving Station lookout tower. Tucker passed the signal on to the keeper (his father, Charles), who quickly went to the lighthouse in the surfboat to see what was going on.

Keeper Tucker had two motorized boats: an eight-horsepower Beebe-McClellan surfboat and the big 34-foot Merryman motor lifeboat named *Success*. The lifeboat was best suited for the rescue, but its motor wasn't working. The early gasoline engines were always less than reliable. The Life-Savers had routinely worked on it all morning, but were unable to repair it. The distance to the *Waldo* was 32 miles and the weather abysmal, with the wind blowing at 50 mph. It would be an extremely difficult and dangerous run for the lifeboat, but near suicidal for the small surfboat. The NOAA weather simulation study showed a maximum wave height during this time of 16 feet![4] The courage it took to venture out in those horrific conditions was incredible. Regardless of the danger, at 2:30 p.m. Keeper Charles A. Tucker ordered the crew to the surfboat and they headed for the *Waldo*. The old Life-Saver's motto said they had to go out. It didn't say anything about coming back. Yet, not a man hesitated or complained. They were professionals. This was their job, something they constantly trained for.

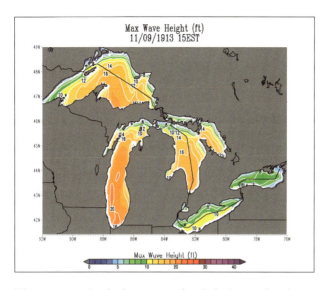

Wave height model of conditions on the Great Lakes, mid-afternoon Sunday, November 9, 1913.
NOAA

The crewmen in the boat were closely knit, too; brothers, cousins, neighbors, all fellow surfmen. They couldn't let their mates down. How could they face them later, or if tragedy struck and a man lost, explain to the families what had happened; that somehow they didn't give it their all?

Thinking of this small surfboat battling though the waves, wind and blizzard, I am reminded of the opening lines to "A Seafarer's Christmas Poem" by Robert Louis Stevenson. Though a bit out of context, it does evoke what it must have been like for the Life-Savers battling onward against the elements.

> The sheets were frozen hard,
> and they cut the naked hand;
> The decks were like a slide,
> where a seaman scarce could stand;
> The wind was a nor'wester,
> blowing squally off the sea;
> And cliffs and spouting breakers
> were the only things a-lee.
> They heard the surf a-roaring
> before the break of day …
> But 'twas only with the peep of Light
> we saw how ill we lay.

It is relatively easy to assign fearlessness to the surfmen, after all they trained together just for such desperate rescues. A powerful bond of camaraderie and mutual dependence glued the crew as one, but what about the families, the wives, mothers, sons and daughters left ashore? What emotions did they feel as their men disappeared into the stormy black lake on a mission they might not return from? A century afterward, the son of Surfman Thomas W. Bennetts remembered, "My dad wouldn't talk about it. My mother did, but he wouldn't."

As the little white surfboat sputtered her way into the storm, two local men safe ashore were supposedly heard to comment, "Boys, you better wire Washington to send another Coast Guard crew. You'll never see this one again. That little boat will never live in this storm."[5] It is worth noting that the surfboats used by the Life-Saving Service were superbly well designed, built and tested. The basic surfboat design came from the small fishing boats used by New Jersey coastal fishermen, launched directly from the beach into the breaking surf and on out to the nets, returning to shore the same way. The service refined it until finally reaching the epitome of design with the model used by the Eagle Harbor crew. The big lifeboats also were highly specialized, the basic design taken from the boats used by Britain's Royal National Lifeboat Institute. Extremely seaworthy, they stood the demanding test of rescue again and again.

The Life-Savers made it about 8 miles before Keeper Tucker reluctantly concluded that conditions were too severe. In the 20-degree temperatures, the surfboat had iced up and was almost unmanageable from the weight, barely responding to the keeper's commands. The men were totally drenched from boarding seas and flying spray and were quickly becoming ineffective due to the cold. The keeper knew that cold robs not only strength, but courage, too. He swung the helm around and started the long run back to the station, arriving about 6:15 p.m. Frozen to their seats and stiff in ice-covered oilskins, the men had to be helped out of the boat by their families,

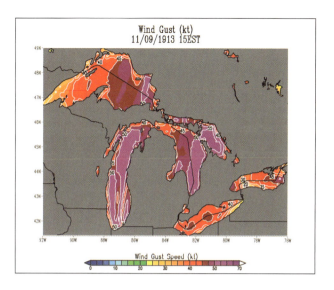

Wind gust model of conditions on the Great Lakes, mid-afternoon Sunday, November 9, 1913.
NOAA

the keeper's wife and young daughters cutting the ice off them before the life jackets could be removed. Walking back to his office, Keeper Tucker noticed that the station wind gauge registered 70 mph! It had been a hell of an effort, but the rescue hadn't been made.

When it learned of the *Waldo* wreck, a Calumet radio station tried to make contact with her. The station was already in contact with other storm-wracked vessels. When its calls went unanswered, the station concluded she was without a wireless. Regardless of the outcome, it was a glimpse of the future.[6]

The dock walloper's hard work finally paid off and the *Smith* had her belly filled with 9,500 tons of ore. When the final shot rumbled into the hold at 4:30 p.m. on Sunday, November 9, Captain Owen was ready to leave, but he waited long enough for a shipment of provisions to arrive from the Rydholm Brothers store. The company supplied most of the boats loading at the city. One of the brothers was Carl, a lake sailor whom Captain Owen knew well.[7]

With the provisions stowed away in the galley, the deckhands hauled aboard the heavy ice-coated hawsers and headed out into the lake. The wind, which had

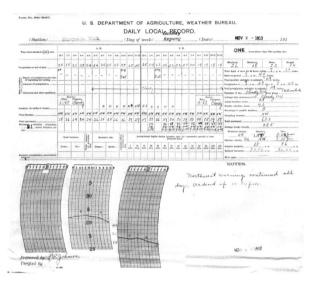

The Marquette weather bureau report for November 9 didn't indicate the horror yet to come. It could be construed as a "sucker hole."

been 30 mph when she left, quickly rose to 44 mph. Apparently Captain Owen thought that the slight lull was proof the storm was breaking. The recordings, however, were taken from the Weather Bureau station in the city. It was blowing far harder on the open lake.

Before leaving Marquette, Captain Owen either forgot or, given the stormy conditions, purposely failed to invite Mr. and Mrs. F.O. Brown to sail to Cleveland with him. Brown was his nephew, in town visiting and expecting to make the trip down with his uncle.[8] The couple would have traveled in the guest suite in the forward deckhouse. By such omissions are lives forever altered.

When the *Smith* left, according to the NOAA simulation estimate, seas offshore were running to a maximum height of 14 feet and the wind gusting hard northwest at roughly 50 mph. Captain Owen knew that it would be a very rough trip for the *Smith* and her crew, but the heavy ore would help to stabilize the ship, and it did look like the weather was finally going to break in his favor. Lake Superior had been blowing a hard northwest storm, but shortly after noon on Sunday, it moderated slightly and the captain, apparently thinking that the storm was over, left for the Soo. Doubtless seas and wind would drop as he made his way down. Freighters didn't

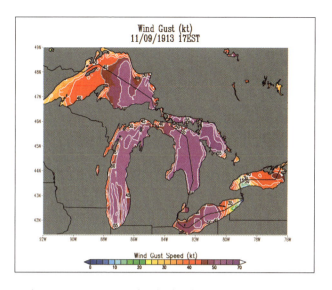

The sea conditions facing the small motor surfboat were terrible with winds of 50 mph. See next page for wave chart.
NOAA

make money sitting at the dock. She was soon past the breakwater bound east for the locks.

Many townspeople watched in awe as the big freighter plowed her way out into the still tumultuous lake. One observer was Captain Charles Fox of the whaleback steamer *Choctaw,* in Marquette waiting to unload coal at the F.B. Spear dock.

The *Choctaw* had her own storm adventure reaching Marquette. She left Ashtabula on the 4th, reaching Lake Huron the next day. Rough conditions lasted throughout the trip north with a constantly changing barometer. Clearing the Soo on the morning of the 7th, things were quiet until past Whitefish Point, when strong south winds slammed her, the barometer dropping to 28.50, a very low reading. Captain Fox kept her close to the shelter of the south shore until reaching Marquette at 2 a.m. on the 8th.

Choctaw started unloading in the morning of the 8th. All went well until the wind picked up again at 4 p.m., and at 9:30 p.m. shifted northwest with heavy snow. At 2:30 a.m. on the 9th, Captain Fox dropped his outboard anchor with a long scope of chain and ran more hawsers to the dock bollards. By 6 a.m., it was so bad that he left the dock anchoring out at the end of the old No. 4 dock

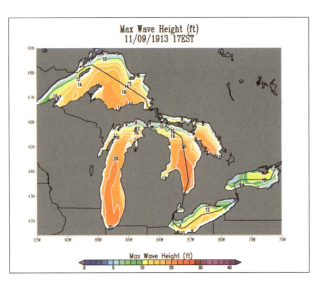

The sea conditions facing the small motor surfboat were terrible with seas cresting at 16 feet. See previous page for wind chart.
NOAA

with 150 feet of new 7-inch line to the end of the dock. He held his secure mooring for nearly two days. The *Choctaw* eventually loaded ore at the Presque Isle dock for her downbound run.

Captain Fox later related to a local paper, "The *Smith* was loaded on the north side of the No. 5 dock. It was necessary to put out his lake line to hold the boat to the dock while loading. He finished loading about 4:30 p.m., left the dock, backed out into the harbor, turned around and went out into the lake. He cleared the breakwater about 5 p.m., headed down the lake, and about 5:20 p.m. changed his course to what I would judge to be about north. At about 5:50 p.m., the mate called my attention to the way he was acting. I looked out and he appeared to be turning around. I do not think I ever saw a vessel roll heavier. After some little time, he got her head to it again and we went to supper. When we came out from supper, she was out of sight."[9]

In a later report to his company, Captain Fox claimed, "It was snowing, which might have obstructed our view. This was perhaps the last seen of the *Henry B. Smith*. With the terrific gale and tremendous sea, I am fully convinced she did not get over 15 or 20 miles out of Marquette."

The whaleback steamer *Choctaw* shelters in Marquette rather than chance the big lake.
HAMILTON COLLECTION/ RUTHERFORD B. HAYES LIBRARY

Whether the crew of the *Smith* was called to supper is unknown, but certainly the rolling and pitching of the ship would have made cooking, serving and eating a normal meal most difficult. Perhaps the best that steward Rufus Judson and second cook Harry Haskin could do was cold sandwiches and hot coffee.

Based on Captain Fox's comments, Captain Owen found the going too tough and headed north for the shelter of Keweenaw Point 60 miles to the west. The rocky Keweenaw Peninsula reaches out into Lake Superior like a skeletal finger 75 miles long. It is still common today for lakers to shelter behind the Keweenaw from strong north storms. Evidently he was trying to shelter behind the Keweenaw the same way the *Waldo* did. The closer the *Smith* got to the point, the greater the protection from the pounding northerly seas. She was in effect running for shelter, but to get there she had to butt her stem into the pounding waves and take their punishment.

According to the papers, sailors on the steamer *Denmark,* safely moored in Marquette Harbor, like the *Choctaw,* noticed something else far more menacing. As the *Smith* was clearing Marquette, her deckhands were still working to secure the hatches. Since the *Smith* had

Keeper Henry Cleary (center front) of the Marquette Life-Saving Service Station.

32 hatches and each required individual attention, it was a long process. Trying to do it with seas rolling down the decks was nearly impossible. There was no mention of how they were securing the hatches. Based on what we know of her hatch system, the best guess was closing the steel leaves. Given the wind and wave conditions, it was a critical job.

Henry Cleary, the longtime keeper of the Marquette Life-Saving Service Station, also watched the *Smith* leave. Seeing her shoulder her way into the big waves, he opined that surely Captain Owen would see the folly of continuing on and return to the safety of Marquette. While Owen likely realized the former, he never did the latter. Cleary's station logbook simply stated that she was "bucking into the teeth of the gale." It was a classic understatement.[10]

Despite the newfangled telephone and older telegraph, Keeper Cleary had no idea of the mounting rescue effort for the *Waldo* crew or anything of the wrecked steamer. The newspapers were far behind events and unless Keeper Tucker needed help from Cleary, there would be no station-to-station contact.

Imagine what it must have been like in the *Smith*'s pilothouse. The wheelsman, Charles Cattanach from Sombra, Ontario, or Edward Shipley from Deckerville, Minnesota, stood with a tight grip on the big wheel, feet braced wide for balance, trying to hold to the given course of 078.5 degrees for Au Sable Point, 60 miles distant. Rounding the Au Sable Point there would be a new heading for Whitefish Point and the Soo. Given the weather situation, both wheelsmen could have been present. On calmer days the wheelsman often perched on a wood stool, but not today, not when the ship was bombarded by greybeards slamming into her constantly.

As the ship ran east, the wind and waves tried to push her south of her course, which meant more port rudder to force the bow northerly and back on track. It was a continuous fight with the storm. Captain Owen would have likely stood behind and to the right of the wheelsman, perhaps with his back braced against the chart table. Like the wheelsman, he kept shifting his attention from the compass course to the progression of steep seas smashing into the ship. Most waves appeared to be about 15 feet or so in height, but periodically a 20-footer rose up to deliver a hull-rattling hammering.

Looking aft out the rear of the pilothouse, Captain Owen noted the heavy spray coming across the weather deck as the deckhands worked with Boatswain Joseph Zink from Corunna, Ontario, to close the last of the hatches. With the pitch and roll of the ship, it was a difficult job, but Captain Owen knew Zink would see it was done right. With what Lake Superior was kicking up, properly closed hatches were vital.

There were other things that Captain Owen made certain of. He passed the order that once the hatches were secured, no one was to go on deck, period. It was too dangerous. All deck openings were to be closed and kept closed, including those to accommodations. The boatswain had already taken care of lashing down all loose gear like mooring lines and steel drums of lubricating oil.

Chief Engineer Charles Rayburn also had a list of must-dos including checking all linkages and controls for steering. All spares had to be secured and a close eye kept on all gauges. Keeping the big triple expansion steam engine going was critical at any time, but especially when bulling your way through a storm. As conditions worsened, he stood by the throttle to react if the pitching of the boat threw the propeller out of the water. A racing shaft and propeller could easily fail or damage the engine with deadly effect.

The engineer relied heavily on his stokers to feed the insatiable boiler fires. No fire, no steam, no power, and the ship and all aboard were bound for old Davy Jones' watery locker. One of the keys to keeping the boilers working was a small glass tube gauge showing the boiler water level. If all the tubes weren't covered with water, the boiler would overheat with catastrophic results. A good stoker always kept one eye on the water gauge. How the stoker fed the fire was vital, too. Coal wasn't shoveled in haphazardly. Each shovel load had to be tossed in just the right location to keep an evenly burning bed of red hot coals on the grate. In a storm like the *Smith* was fighting, with the slippery steel deck heaving and pitching, successfully feeding the beast was most difficult.

Fair winds and calm seas may be every captain's wish, but it wasn't to be for Captain Owen on this trip. The farther east the *Smith* went, the worse the weather became. Captain Owen knew he had erred in leaving shelter when he did, but that was spilled milk now. He had been fooled by the sucker hole just like any rookie! With the way the wind was gusting, he would never be able to get back into Marquette and safely anchor. His only choice was to change course to the north and head for the shelter of the Keweenaw Peninsula. Pulling the stopper out of the brass speaking tube to the engine room, he whistled up Chief Engineer Rayburn and told him to stand by. He was going to ring down for full power when he made the turn to port and wanted everything the chief had.

The *Henry B. Smith* was no match for the fury of Superior.
EDWARD PUSICK COLLECTION

When he turned, the ship would show her bilge to the sky and anything not secured was going to go a-tumbling, including his crew. But there was no way he could warn everyone, so all he could do was hope they would find something solid to hang on to. His crew had been in heavy weather before. They knew what was coming.

Checking again that Bosun Zink and his men were clear of the deck, Captain Owen began to study the waves closely, looking for a series of smaller waves to turn against. He didn't want to butt into a big 20-footer. He needed to turn as fast as he could to avoid getting caught in the trough between two waves or heeling over enough to capsize. The big lakers had enough engine power when going straight ahead, but making a quick turn into the tumbling seas was always a very dicey maneuver. Seeing his chance, Captain Owen ordered, "Hard a Port!" and the big steamer slowly and ponderously swung around to the left, although rolling to an ungodly angle before coming back up and straightening on a northerly heading. This was the turn that Captain Fox on the *Choctaw* had observed. The *Smith* was now taking the seas on her nose as she struggled for the Keweenaw. Considering the visual distance in the storm, he was likely not more than 5 miles off shore.

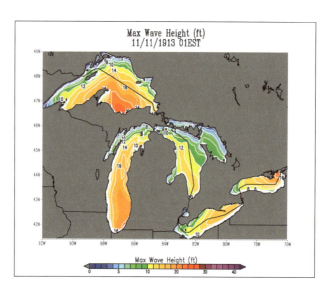

The Eagle Harbor Life-Saving Service crew still faced horrendous conditions and high waves.
NOAA

The previous description is, of course, speculation since there are no witnesses to what actually occurred, but based on normal operating procedure of the period, I believe it to be reasonably accurate.

Immediately on their return to Eagle Harbor, Keeper Tucker put No. 1 Surfman Anthony F. Glaza and Machinist's Mate Surfman Thomas W. Bennetts to work on the lifeboat engine.[11] The remainder of the crew went to warm up and get what rest was possible until the keeper launched another effort. After working nonstop through the night and the following day, the two men came through, coaxing the reluctant engine to coughing life.

As soon as possible Keeper Tucker called his crew and after midnight Tuesday, November 11, *Success* came thundering down the steel rails into the harbor. The storm had moderated a bit, the NOAA simulation suggests winds north, gusting 35 mph and maximum waves of 16 feet, mountainous to the small lifeboat. Shouldering her way into the cold seas, the 34-foot motor lifeboat *Success* churned her way toward Keweenaw Point. Spray turned to ice on her decks. Rails and lines froze to the deck, having to be pried loose when needed. Surfmen huddled out of the worst of the wind and seas behind the small canvas dodger, but the bitter cold was

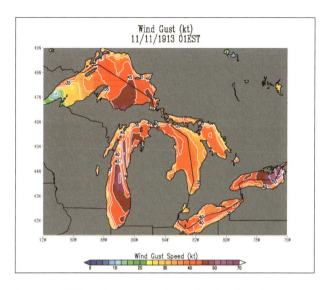

Three days into the storm, winds continued strong.
NOAA

intense, chilling them to the bone despite their heavy wool clothing and oilskins. With Keeper Tucker at the helm, the lonely lifeboat drove on and on into the black night, climbing one sea and smashing hard into another, bombarded with snow and lashed by freezing wind.

Keeper Tucker's crew wasn't alone on the lake. Around noon on Monday, the 10th, he telephoned the Portage Life-Saving Station and Keeper Thomas McCormick alerting them to the rescue effort. Portage Station was located on the Portage Lake Ship Canal, 80 miles to the south of Gull Rock Reef. McCormick also could have been notified by the *Stephenson*. After the first mate contacted Eagle Harbor, Captain Mosher was concerned enough about the wrecked crew that he later sent the second mate ashore to find out what was happening. When the mate discovered that the Eagle Harbor crew had failed in their first effort, he called the Portage Station, too, thus helping set in motion the second crew.

The quickest route from the Portage Station to the *Waldo* was 60 miles – west to the Upper Entry of the canal, then right along the Keweenaw Peninsula to the wreck. Running east through the canal to Keweenaw Bay and north under the lee of the Keweenaw was longer by 20 miles, but was far more protected and it was likely

The old Portage Life-Saving Service Station was the launch point for many thrilling rescues.

MICHIGAN TECHNOLOGICAL UNIVERSITY ARCHIVES

that they could make better time, plus the chances of surviving the trip were far greater. But 60 miles is shorter than 80, so Keeper McCormick initially tried to run the open lake. After about a mile, he realized it wasn't going to work. Deciding on the longer but potentially faster route, he ran his 36-foot Type E lifeboat *Champion* down to the Lower Entry where Captain Bert Nelson and the 99-foot, 500-horsepower tug *Daniel Hebard* of nearby Pequaming, Michigan, took her in tow for Gull Rock. Using the tug would speed the trip.

During the run north, although they were relatively protected, waves broke over the lifeboat continually. And the hammering from the seas eventually caused her to leak badly. Although it was self-bailing, the outlet valves iced up and had to be constantly chopped open to allow the water to drain. A heavy layer of ice also formed on the decks making her list heavily and difficult to handle. Like *Success*, her lines froze in place and had to be pried off by the crew.

Even when towed, Life-Service regulations required that the lifeboat be at least partially manned, with enough men aboard to handle the situation if a towing hawser parted or the boat had to be cast adrift. A crewman also always had a hatchet handy, prepared to cut the hawser quickly if needed. Except for the hatchet man, all others rode in the stern to keep the weight aft. Under the storm conditions it was a miserable ride, the stern constantly wet from spray and ice.

Prior to the lifeboat being taken under tow by the *Hebard*, the Keweenaw Central Railroad was preparing a special train to run down to Houghton and take the Life-Savers and their equipment to Bete Grise, 45 miles to the north. But Keeper McCormick decided that the tug was probably the faster option and potentially less damaging to the boat. Lifting the heavy boat on and off the railcar, properly securing it and launching it at Bete Grise were all steps fraught with potential for damage. And a damaged boat could end the rescue attempt.

Captain Thomas McCormick of Portage Life-Saving Station.
KEWEENAW COUNTY HISTORICAL SOCIETY, MARITIME COMMITTEE

Soon after the *Smith*'s departure from Marquette, the lull ended and the storm attacked with renewed fury. Several of the ships that survived the storm claimed wind speeds in excess of 70 mph. The storm continued to howl through Sunday night and into Monday.

Marquette weather station observer P.E. Johnson recorded the temperature plummeting to 18 degrees that night with a blizzard of snow battering the area. Ishpeming, just 14 miles inland from the city, had 6- to 9-foot snow drifts. Everywhere, citizens hunkered down to wait out the storm.

Heading for the Keweenaw required Captain Owen to take the waves right on the *Smith*'s nose, resulting in mountains of water smashing onto the foredeck and sweeping down the length of the open weather deck, tearing and grasping at each of the hastily secured hatch covers before battering into the aft cabin, a sequence repeated again and again. Looking forward out his pilothouse windows, all Captain *Smith* saw was the white

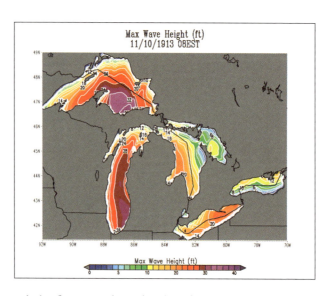

The *Smith* steamed into the building monster. Lake Superior truly became a sailor's hell.
NOAA

splash of water striking the glass, faintly illuminated by the dim glow of the binnacle lamp. Otherwise, it was utter blackness, not a star or moon to give any hope that there was a world beyond the darkened pilothouse.

The power of the storm continued to grow with tons of water pouring over her deck. As she lurched on through the waves, it was impossible for a man to venture on deck, let alone work. "The hatches; Lord pray the hatches stay secure!"

As he fought his way to the shelter of the Keweenaw, the waves grew larger and more powerful. According to the NOAA simulation, by 8 p.m. on Sunday, November 9, the maximum were 24 feet; by 2 a.m. on Monday it was 28 feet; by 6 a.m. 30 feet and two hours later 32 feet! How long the *Smith* stayed afloat is unknown, but clearly the chances of her survivability decreased as time passed. The NOAA simulation showed different areas of the lake having varying weather conditions, though all were characterized as staggeringly horrible. While the area that the *Smith* was sailing in was generally hammered by 60-mph gusts around 4 a.m. on Sunday (if she was still afloat), at nearly the same time, the captain of the steamer *Harvester* reported gusts of 100 mph just west of Michipicoten Island in the eastern lake.

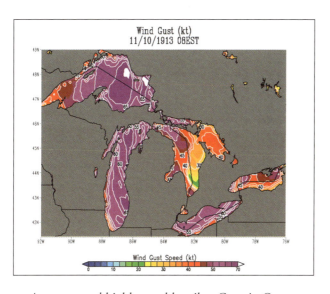

    A veteran and highly capable sailor, Captain Owen fought the storm with all of his substantial skill, but was losing the battle in the increasing maelstrom. His standing rigging was screaming from the rising wind. Soon it was howling, a chorus suitable for a priestly choir from the Spanish Inquisition, intended to drown out the terrible screams of their innocent and helpless victims. Once the hatch covers started to loosen, the fight was over. If the covers breached during darkness, Captain Owen likely never would have known, unable to see the black deck stretching behind him. Although his generator provided electric power for deck lights, nearly all were smashed already by the waves.
    The surging water searched out every weakness, flooding into the cargo holds with every passing wave. Although the engineers kept their big steam pumps clanging away at full capacity, they couldn't expel the water quickly enough as it poured through smashed stern cabin doors and down deep into the engine room and bilges. Waves ripped doors off their hinges, skylights and portholes stove, and bulkheads knocked asunder. The lifeboats were long since swept off their davits and blown into the lake. Losing the lifeboats made no difference anyway. There wasn't a boat made that could survive

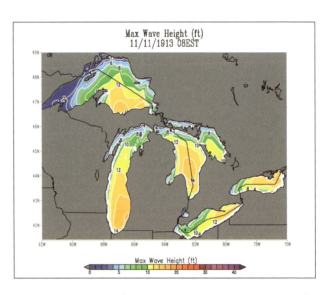

The NOAA simulation indicated 35 mph winds and 16-foot waves when the lifeboat battled for Keweenaw Point.
NOAA

the terrible uproar of wind and water or crew capable of launching one in the screaming storm anyway. The end for the *Smith* and her crew was coming soon.

As the *Smith* was dying, chewed to pieces by the fury of the storm, the crew of the *Waldo* was staring death in the face too. But death, for them would blink.

The Life-Saving Service crew from Eagle Harbor didn't give up after failing to reach the *Waldo* in their surfboat. At 7 a.m., Tuesday the 11th, the big lifeboat *Success* arrived at the wreck as the first gray streaks of another stormy dawn were painting the sky. In front of her was the broken and ice-covered *Waldo*. Keeper Tucker and his crew were soon joined by Keeper McCormick and his Portage crew in their lifeboat *Champion*. It took them 14 hours to get to the wreck, arriving at 3 a.m. Since it was too dark to see anything, they sheltered behind the point until daylight.

The U.S. Life-Saving Service *Annual Report* for 1914 recorded the drama of the lifeboat's arrival at the wreck. "The imperiled company had caught no glimpse of a ship since a steamer passed them in the early hours of their misfortune, apparently leaving them to their fate. They had now ceased to hope that assistance would come to

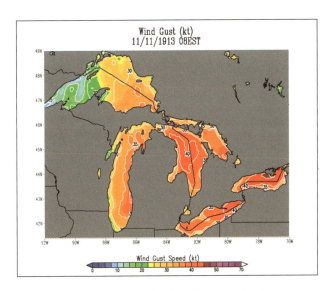

them. Their surprise may be therefore imagined, when looking out from their shelter, they held in the morning light of the 11th a grotesque ghostly shape top a wave, poise on its crest for a moment, then sink out of sight as the wave slipped from under it and went racing on. When the object again came into view it was nearer, and the mystery was explained and with understanding the watchers felt the warming blood leap in their chilled veins. It was an ice-covered boat, its white bow bearing the emblem of the U.S. Life-Saving Service."

When the Portage crew worked its way to within hailing distance of the *Waldo*, a crewman on the wreck yelled for the boat to stand clear until they could chop themselves free. Every door and hatch on the steamer was iced shut, clad in thick white armor. The *Success* arrived a few minutes later and, not having heard the *Waldo* crewman's yell, went directly to the wreck. *Success* was a mirror image of the Portage boat, covered in shimmering ice.

The lake was still extremely rough. As waves were breaking hard on the hull of the *Waldo,* she offered little protection for the lifeboats coming alongside. The water around the steamer was shoal and littered with rocks. Regardless of the clear danger to themselves, both

The *Turret Chief* ashore on the Keweenaw.

MICHIGAN TECHNOLOGICAL UNIVERSITY ARCHIVES

lifeboats laid up to the *Waldo*. With great dexterity, Surfman John Beck climbed onto the ice castle to help with the evacuation. Other surfmen soon joined him aboard the dead steamer.

They found the windlass room encased in ice up to 2 feet thick. Chopping through to free the sailors took considerable work from outside and inside. *Success* ended up taking 13 men, two women and the ship's dog aboard. Some of the sailors climbed down a rope ladder. Others jumped from the deck into the bobbing lifeboat, their fall cushioned by the Life-Savers below. Icy spray from the waves smashing into the *Waldo* constantly rained down on everyone. The two women had to be bodily thrown from the steamer into the lifeboat and caught by the surfmen. Lifeboats rising and falling violently as the swells passed beneath made the loading very difficult. The Portage boat, *Champion,* picked up nine men.[12]

The survivors were in very poor shape, nearly frozen from their long ordeal. Eagle Harbor surfman Anthony Glaza later wrote, "Some had towels wrapped around their heads, and some were wearing socks for mittens. The majority had neither. We put our mackinaws and caps on them until we could get them to the tug. The women cried for joy when we wrapped them up in warm blankets, and when we put them on the tug they offered a prayer of thanksgiving and asked the blessing of heaven up our captain and crew."

The *Hebard* was anchored just a few miles to the west of the wreck in Keystone Bay. The heated cabin of the tug provided vital salvation to both the rescued and rescuers. Hot food and drink helped, too. The *Waldo* survivors hadn't eaten in 90 hours and the 100 pounds of ham and crate of eggs that the tug had aboard was a banquet for the famished crew. As soon as things were squared away, the tug took the *Champion* in tow, arriving at Hancock, Michigan, at 5 p.m. Back at the station the Portage crew discovered the lifeboat's stem had been damaged, likely while striking hard against the steamer's steel hull in the wave surge while loading survivors from the wreck.

For the *Smith,* the end game proved tragic. Roughly 36 miles south-southeast from Keweenaw Point, she plunged to the bottom, taking all hands down with her. The precise time of loss is unknown as is the date. It is surmised either late on Saturday, November 9, or early Sunday morning. Fate is indeed the hunter.

But there is what might have been. Had the dock crew in Marquette been able to load her on Saturday and had Captain Owen decided to head for the Soo immediately, and had he experienced the same weather once outside the harbor, he likely would have turned west-northwest for the Keweenaw. Would he have spotted the *Waldo* on Gull Rock, or even the tug *Hebard* towing the Portage Life-Savers north? Indeed, could Captain Owen have taken Mosher's place in the story, setting in motion the wheels of help? If somehow he was able to survive the horrific trip from Marquette, would he have ended up on one of the Keweenaw's deadly reefs or even plowed dead ashore? Regardless of the world of might-have-been, one crew lived and one crew died.

The Eagle Harbor crew wasn't finished with their lifesaving work, however. On their long miserable run back to the station, they discovered the wreck of the steel turret steamer *Turret Chief* ashore east of Copper

The Eagle Harbor crew after their return from the *Waldo* wreck. Note the iced-over clothing.

Harbor. During the trip out, they had missed it in the inky blackness. Only after landing and assuring that the steamer's crew was safe did the Life-Savers resume their trip home.

The *Turret Chief,* Captain Thomas Paddington, a British-built 257-foot steel turret steamer, was upbound when caught by the maw of the storm. Unable to make headway against the seas, she was just marking time before heading for the bottom. So much water had flooded her, it was a bare 2 inches from her boilers when the engineers drew the fires to prevent an explosion. In her case being blown ashore on the Keweenaw was a godsend. In fact, she was so far up on the rocks that her bow was a mere 20 feet off the beach. Using ropes and ladders, the 18-man crew quickly abandoned her, fearing immediate breakup. But in their pell-mell rush to get off the ship, they brought no food or supplies of any kind, including heavy clothing. Once they realized that the boat was going to stay intact, they tried to climb back aboard, but the heavy coating of ice made it impossible.

They were resourceful, however, building hasty shelters from driftwood and pine boughs. Hungry and freezing to death, they could but huddle around their

This photo of Marquette's 36-foot motor lifeboat following a 1920s rescue well illustrates what the Eagle Harbor lifeboat would have looked like on return to the station.

fire. They had no idea where they were, other than shipwrecked somewhere on Lake Superior's desolate shores. After a couple of days, a group of Native Americans found them and brought the cold, hungry and bedraggled sailors to Copper Harbor.

All during the Life-Savers' return to Eagle Harbor the weather was very bad and *Success* was leaking continuously. When they reached the station and hauled the boat up the railway and into the boathouse, they found her filled with water to the deck. The constant pounding of the four-hour run split the portside air tanks, causing them to flood. That the Life-Savers made it back at all is strong testament to the inherent strength of the Service lifeboats.

The old Life-Saving Service crews had immense, nearly religious faith in their lifeboats, which was evident in the names: *Success* – Eagle Harbor, *Champion* – Portage, *Loyal* – Grand Marais, *Tempest* – Marquette, to name but a few. Regardless of the ferocity of the storm, the men just knew that their boat would get them home. They trusted them implicitly. The waterlogged condition of *Success* was proof positive that she would always come through.

The Eagle Harbor crew in their trusty lifeboat.

While the crews tended to look at the rescue as just part of what was expected, others recognized their accomplishment, including Secretary of the Treasury William Gibbs McAdoo, who sent a personal letter of congratulations to the keepers.[13] The Life-Saving Service was under the Treasury Department.

In recognition of their heroic rescue, both Portage and Eagle Harbor crews were awarded Gold Life-Saving Medals. It was only the fourth instance in the 44-year history of the Service such a double award was made. Previous double awards went to Chadwick's (Green Island) and Mantoloking (Swan Point) stations, New Jersey, for the February 1880 rescue of the crew of schooner *George Tulane*; Tatham's and Avalon stations (also New Jersey) for the December 1912 rescue of the crew of the steamer *Margaret;* and Cape Disappointment and Point Adams stations, Oregon, for the January 1913 attempted rescue of the steamer *Rosecrans* crew.

Awarded July 15, 1914
Charles A. Tucker – Keeper, Eagle Harbor
Anthony F. Glaza – No. 1 Surfman, Eagle Harbor
Thomas W. Bennetts – No. 2 Surfman, Eagle Harbor
Serge Anderson – No. 3 Surfman, Eagle Harbor
John Beck – No. 4 Surfman, Eagle Harbor
George Holpainen – No. 5 Surfman, Eagle Harbor
Chester Tucker – No. 6 Surfman, Eagle Harbor

This Gold Life-Saving Medal was awarded to Keeper Charles A. Tucker of Eagle Harbor.

Charles Kumpula – No. 7 Surfman, Eagle Harbor
Henry Padberg – No. 8 Surfman, Eagle Harbor
Thomas H. McCormick – Keeper, Portage
John McDonald – No. 1 Surfman, Portage
John C. Alfsen – No. 2 Surfman, Portage
Fred C. Sollman – No. 3 Surfman, Portage
Paul Liedtke – No. 4 Surfman, Portage
Collin S. Westrope – No. 5 Surfman, Portage
David M. Small – No. 6 Surfman, Portage
Oscar Marshall – No. 7 Surfman (temporary), Portage

The *Waldo* proved a constructive total loss and was abandoned to the underwriters. The following year the wreck was purchased for $10,000, refloated and rebuilt at the American Ship Building yard at Lorain, Ohio. With her new name, *Riverton,* she sailed until wrecking in Georgian Bay in 1943. Again she was recovered, rebuilt and renamed, becoming the *Mohawk Deer*. She sank in 1967 while under tow to the scrap yard in Italy.

At Keeper Charles Tucker's retirement dinner, he was asked where he found the courage to go out into the hurricane-whipped lake to make the rescue. The old Life-Saver just replied that it was his job. Pressed further about concerns for his own safety, he just said, "the manual didn't say anything about that." It was just a variation of the old Life-Savers motto: "Regulations say we have to go out. ..."

Chapter 7

Picking Up the Pieces

Although folks at Marquette expressed fear for the safety of the *Smith,* the maritime community as a whole wasn't worried until Thursday, November 13, when she was officially overdue at the Soo. The owners wired every port on the lake inquiring as to the *Smith*'s whereabouts, but all came back negative. No one had seen the *Smith* after hauling out of Marquette.

Some confusion reigned, however, when the captain of the steamer *Miller* reported seeing the *Smith* pull into Bete Grise for shelter, but it turned out it was the *Stephenson* instead. Another master thought that he saw her entering the St. Marys River, but it, too, was a case of mistaken steamer. Another rumor circulated that there were two steamers ashore on Michipicoten Island. Maybe the *Smith* was one of them. But nothing was ashore at Michipicoten. It was all just wishful thinking.

Meanwhile, at Marquette, clear proof of an unidentified steamer wreck began to wash up on the beaches. The first wreckage came ashore near the Presque Isle ore dock 2 miles to the north of the Lower Harbor, from which the *Smith* departed. Consisting of oak paneling, bits and pieces of furniture and small sections of wood, it was definitely from a steamer. But was it from the *Smith*?

Keeper Henry Cleary carefully examined it and thought at least some was from the *Smith,* but likely most came from the wreck of the *L.C. Waldo* breaking apart on Gull Rock Reef at the tip of the Keweenaw.[1] By now the newspapers were filled with the story of dramatic rescue of the *Waldo* crew, so Cleary was familiar with the overall situation. The *Waldo* was a well known boat in Marquette, often loading at both the Presque Isle and downtown docks.

The news became more ominous when the steamer *Frontenac* docked on Wednesday, November 12 and the captain reported that one of his oilers saw a body floating in a life belt 11 miles east of the city. Rough seas made recovery impossible. Apparently the body never came ashore. Was the floater from the *Smith*? Perhaps it was even from the *Leafield*? Apparently none of her crew were ever recovered.[2]

On Thursday, November 13, landlooker Dan Johnson came into Marquette carrying an oar marked *Henry B. Smith*. He said he found it, as well as three others and part of a pike pole marked "*Henry,*" between the Chocolay River and Shot Point just east of the city. The entire area was also littered with small pieces of wreckage, evidently from the upper works of a steamer. Was it from the *Smith* or *Waldo* or both? Past Shot Point, the beach was filled with more wreckage including part of a white deckhouse. White was the color of the *Smith*'s house.[3] Johnson stated that the wreckage looked like it had been on the beach for a long time, suggesting it likely came ashore on Monday.

In the days following, more reports of wreckage reached the city. William Powell, a fisherman living at Powell's Point near Munising, reported finding flotsam while in his fishing boat below the Pictured Rocks. He brought several pieces back with him including a built-in companionway stenciled in red "*Henry B. Smith,*" a marked oar, two cabin doors (white outside and grained inside), two screens for port and starboard running lights, two bed pillows, a green corduroy cushion and an armful of unused life belts. The wreckage was scattered as far as Beaver Lake, 16 miles east of Munising. By appearance, it all came from the *Smith*. Marine men guessed that the steamer's superstructure was battered to pieces by the waves, either while actually sinking or before. Additional wreckage was found on the west and north sides of

Grand Island.[4] Clearly, however, a considerable amount of the wreckage was from the *Waldo*, an older boat with far more wooden superstructure than the all-steel *Smith*.

Beach patrols east of Marquette continued to find more wreckage, including wooden hatch covers. The wooden covers are a bit puzzling, since the *Smith* had telescoping steel covers. Some of the wreckage, including glass fragments from her head lamps, stanchions and a piece of door, were brought to the city and displayed in several storefronts. It was, after all, good advertising! If people came to look at the wreckage, perhaps they could be tempted into the store, too.[5]

Although thorough searches were made for bodies, none were ever found ashore, at least not between Marquette and Grand Island. Keeper Cleary knew that the searches would be fruitless, relating, "The chances are that the wind changed before the bodies reached shore thus causing them to drift back to sea. Wreckage such as oars, timbers and doors is light and would float more rapidly reaching the shore before the wind shifted. It is my belief that if bodies of the unfortunate seamen are to be found, they will be picked up on the sands of Grand Island or perhaps as far south as Whitefish Point."

Only two of the bodies of the estimated 26 crewmen were ever found.[6] The first was that of the second cook Harry Haskin, found by the *Saxona* 50 miles west of Whitefish Point. He was only identified by a letter in his pocket. His remains were returned to Sandusky for burial.[7] The second body was found in May the following year, frozen in a block of ice near Goulais Point in the eastern lake. Badly decomposed, it was identified as the third engineer John Gallagher, also only by the papers in his pocket and an inscribed watch. There was an unsubstantiated claim that two more were discovered on the beach at Grand Marais, Michigan. Cleary was, of course, correct.[8]

Shortly after midnight November 20, the U.S. Revenue Marine Cutter *Tuscarora* rounded Marquette breakwater and dropped her hook. She was on a relief mission to scout the American shore, including Isle

Royale, searching for the shipwreck and remains. Since the cutter was wireless equipped, it was expected that she would immediately flash the discovery of the *Smith*. It was a fruitless mission.[9]

The Zenith Steamship Company *Saxona* recovered the body of the *Smith*'s second cook.

The Lake Carriers' Association, the trade group of vessel owners and operators, asked local game wardens and deer hunters to keep their eyes open for any bodies if they went anywhere near the beach. The Lake Carriers considered it important to return remains to loved ones, if possible. The search proved fruitless. The rumor that two bodies came ashore near Grand Marais, Michigan, apparently proved groundless.[10]

Ironically, one of the crew did survive. Second Mate John Burke left the ship in Marquette with a severe case of pneumonia. Think of the terrible shock to all the family members, including Burke's wife. When word of the loss of the *Smith* with her entire crew was telegraphed to her, it left no doubt that John was dead. Imagine her astonishment when she received a second telegram, not from the company, but from her "dead" husband announcing his safety. Very ill and needing his wife's kindly care, he left the ship in Marquette and took the train to Sault Ste. Marie, where he transferred to another train and another until finally reaching Cleveland and home. Interviewed later, he sympathized with his lost crew, stating, "It's awful the way men struggle for life when death stares them in the face. God help those poor fellows. I know how it was with the wind and sleet blowing in their faces, beating the breath out of them for hours before the end came. The horror of shipwreck is in the waiting. Pray for sudden and not the grinding, warping, twisting thing called drowning."[11]

Burke's wife told the interviewer that her thoughts and prayers were with Mrs. Owen. "It's hard for her, the heartbroken woman, who scans the lake with tear-dimmed eyes." Her concern would fit all the victims' family members. After her loss, Mrs. Owen lived with the Adams family, one of the owners of the *Smith*, for a number of years. On a trip to California in 1928 to visit her sister, she became ill and died. She wanted to be cremated and her ashes scattered in Lake Superior to be nearer her husband, but as families are wont to do, her sister apparently objected and, while she was cremated, her ashes were placed in a crypt in Forest Lawn Glendale, far from the icy depths of Lake Superior and her true love.

When it was clear that the *Smith* was missing, Mrs. John Gallagher, wife of Third Engineer John Gallagher, and her five small children arrived in Marquette from Escanaba. Family friend Morris Call escorted her. While she was at first confident that her husband would be found alive, as the days passed hope faded into grim reality.[12] John's body wasn't found until the following May.

But where were the bodies of the crew? Many of those from the Lake Huron wrecks eventually drifted ashore. Why didn't those of the *Smith*? A possible explanation for the lack of bodies, other than that expressed by Keeper Cleary, is that the wind and waves created such havoc along the south shore that the waterline was abruptly changed. Entire stretches of swamp and bayou were filled in with sand, making it, in time, into a solid mass of land. The *Smith*'s wreckage was also found higher up the beach, indicating that it came ashore at the height of the storm when the waves were at their largest. Bodies driven ashore at the same time could have been buried in the sand, hidden forever.[13]

Based on the *Fitzgerald* wreck, I assume anyone in the pilothouse was literally washed out when the *Smith* dove for the bottom. This means Captain Owen, the wheelsman and perhaps another man are potentially lost in the mud bottom somewhere near the wreck site. After a century, there should be little of them left.

The remaining crewmen are likely still inside the steamer at whatever duty station is applicable. This isn't unlike the *Fitzgerald* scenario. To this extent the wreck is indeed a gravesite, but not unlike the hundreds of other Great Lakes shipwrecks where loss of life occurred.

It is also reasonable to assume that the *Smith* sank so quickly, the majority of the crew had no time to don life belts. The belts should have kept the bodies afloat long enough to reach shore or be recovered by other ships. Accepting this idea, many of the men are still trapped in the wreck.

Meanwhile, Great Lakes mariners and the Lake Carriers' Association looked for someone to blame for the carnage. The good folks at the U.S. Weather Bureau were an easy scapegoat. The Weather Bureau, in the shipping community's eyes, failed to provide adequate warnings of the ferocity of the storm, especially during the critical November 7 to 9 period. While they posted the "appropriate" warnings, they failed to adequately convey the power of the storm. For example, the criteria for advisories/warnings on the Great Lakes were essentially limited to:

    <u>Warning Wind (knots)</u>
    Small Craft Advisory 18 to 33
    Gale Warning 34 to 47
    Storm Warning 48 or greater

Considering that the wind in many places blew in excess of 60 knots with some areas exceeding 78 knots, mariners had a point. The storm clearly met the criteria for a hurricane, but, of course, hurricanes don't happen on the Great Lakes, so the Weather Bureau bureaucracy refused to consider such a description. Hurricanes are tropical storms, not Great Lakes storms. However, the Weather Bureau's own published criteria authorized such a determination and appropriate warnings for the lakes. It was an epic SNAFU[14] on the part of the Weather Bureau. Of course, this discussion is ancillary to whether the vessels' masters would have believed such a warning and taken suitable action or not. Eventually the Weather Bureau changed its categories, somewhat. An adjusted Gale Warning category for winds of 33 to 48 knots was added. Anything greater than 55 knots was now a Storm

Warning. Hurricane winds, however, still didn't exist on the lakes.

There were numerous examples of the warning flags not flying. When Captain W.T. Mooney was unloading coal from his steamer *Andaste* at Sault Ste. Marie, Michigan, on November 9, he went up to the canal office to check on the weather. As soon as possible he wanted to get under way for Alpena. No signals were flying on the locks, but a captain coming up told him conditions on Lake Huron were "rotten." The weather crew said that the north winds would soon be diminishing. Luckily Captain Mooney decided to anchor above DeTour for the night. Between 11 p.m. and midnight, it blew harder than he had ever experienced.[15]

The fight over whether the storm was a hurricane was just a preliminary round. The main event was yet to come, and it was a true heavyweight bout. Congressman William Gordon of Ohio stepped into the ring, ostensibly to determine if the proper warnings were posted, a pretty tame jab rapidly followed by a hard right. Ringside reporters happily scribbled away as he intoned, "The government is spending great sums of money to conduct the Weather Bureau. We have a right to expect accurate and adequate services from it. If these charges are true, the Bureau is menace to navigation rather than a help to the navigator." Gordon knew his way in the political ring. Hit 'em in the budget!

The Bureau, as a subsidiary of the U.S. Department of Agriculture, knew its way around a political ring, too, parrying the Gordon right with the announcement that it would conduct its own investigation. The chief forecaster in Cleveland, William H. Alexander, who had the responsibility of actually issuing the warning to shipping, was ordered to write a report.

Alexander took the atypical step of speaking directly to local reporters, something the stodgy U.S. Weather Bureau would never allow. Under normal circumstances, such an example of independence and initiative would have destroyed his career. (I suspect he was given a secret okay for this action.) He claimed, "Daring disregard of government storm signals are the main cause of the latest disasters on the Great Lakes. Had the same storm prevailed in foreign waters with government storm signals placed in every port three days ahead of the storm, sounding the warning, a catastrophe never would have happened."

He then took out the knife and jabbed it deep into shippers and captains. "It seems singular to me that lake captains should take their ships out in the face of the warnings. They might have avoided the loss of lives and property and it seems as though the disaster was almost without excuse."[16]

Now the folks sitting around the ring, ship owners and captains, became involved. They yelled out that the warnings were grossly inadequate for the size and power of the storm. They should have been hurricane warnings. (You can almost hear the chant, "Hurricane, Hurricane.") Had they been flying at the signal hoists, we would have kept our ships safe in port. The Weather Bureau played us false. They had a signal for hurricane, and the storm clearly reached that standard, but the bureau refused to call it what it was.

The referees to this fight took note of the public reaction and graded accordingly. The fight had moved out of the ring now. And the shippers and captains were, in the main, correct. Official Weather Bureau publications did include hurricane as a proper signal for the lakes when conditions warranted as they clearly did in this instance. So what happened? Why were the hurricane signals not hoisted?

It seems that the Weather Bureau had been caught in an internal time warp of sorts. It knew that as a new "science" (this is of course still highly debatable), they needed to be precise in all things, especially terminology. And "hurricane" was a term they would only apply to a tropical storm, not a blow on the lakes, regardless of intensity. That the leadership of the bureau hadn't bothered to pass the word to the field or withdraw and change published materials was unimportant. Washington always knows what is best!

Owners and captains were adamant that a proper warning, namely the use of the hurricane flag, would have kept them in port and avoided the deaths and property loss. They also lobbied for local forecasters to have the authority to issue local forecasts more accurately, warning of dangerous conditions. Shippers and captains believed that they should have received the "hurricane" warnings not later than noon on Saturday. There was no sense of urgency for Washington to get them the information they critically needed.

Meanwhile back in the boxing ring, Gordon threw another jab, this one an official notification to President Wilson that he was investigating Mr. Wilson's Weather Bureau. Stung by the jab, Wilson punched back with a weak left-right combination that he would be investigating Great Lakes ship owners and reviewing the policy of allowing ships to sail into the "dangerous" weather season past the end of traditional navigation. Mr. Wilson couldn't allow blame to be attached to his administration. The combination missed the mark widely, just toothless political threats.

But the specters of 250 dead sailors couldn't be wished away by Wilson or ignored by the bureaucrats of the Weather Bureau. Gordon's punches, backed by the jeering crowd, knocked the Weather Bureau to its knees and a technical knockout.

On November 18, the bureau issued an official statement from Washington taking full responsibility for all of the forecasts from November 8 onward. In part it said, "The records show that every Weather Bureau took precautions. Signals were displayed at 112 points along the lakeshore, including 19 Weather Bureau stations from any one of which special information could be had upon request. The severity of the storm was fully recognized by officials in Washington and no information concerning it was concealed or withheld." The Bureau also claimed forecasters had issued correct warnings under existing regulations. (They dodged the question of whose regulations, the unpublished ones in Washington or the ones still current in the field.) Likewise, there was no mention of the forbidden word "hurricane." On command, the stations hoisted the flags during the day and lanterns at night. And sailors died.

Regarding using the word "hurricane," perhaps Captain W.T. Mooney of the steamer *Andaste* summed up the mariners' frustration when he said, "Two hours before the big blow hit the lakes" he received a weather forecast at Detroit: "Moderate northwest winds, diminishing."[17]

The point that came out clearly to all (less to Mr. Wilson and his cronies) was that even when the boys in the forecast shop clearly knew the severity of the storm, regulations by signal prevented them from telling anyone any really useful information. And, in point of fact, the bureau was one move behind the storm, never able to get in front of what was happening. In their defense, without the modern tools available to the forecaster today – computers, satellite monitoring, automated station data feed and a far better understanding of the physical world – it was more black art than science, regardless of the cloak of omnipotent knowledge that Washington tried to hide behind. Today ships big and small receive their weather data via radio or satellite. Condition information at various collection points, such as buoys, is real time. Large commercial operators often use private weather services to analyze data and provide ancillary opinions to the government services. It is a far different weather world than in 1913. Like a century ago, weather forecasting is still critical to the mariner.

A smaller and less bloody debate also raged in Canada following the 1913 storm, with Canadian forecasters lamenting that captains ignored warnings for "heavy gale" and sailed anyway. We warned them. What more can we do?

So, given that as science marched on and weather forecasting improved, U.S. Great Lakes meteorologists can still not issue hurricane warnings, that remains strictly for the sunny Caribbean and Atlantic, but they can issue warnings for "hurricane force winds." Please don't ask me why. It is an unfathomable mystery of weather gods in D.C. Canadian forecasters may also use the phrase as needed.

Storm signal flags were discontinued by the National Weather Service in 1989. Given modern technology, they were no longer deemed efficient. However, the U.S. Coast Guard continues their display flags at many stations as well as marinas, private yacht clubs and mooring areas. They certainly are not as effective as radio alerts, but do serve as a jarring visual reminder of the forecasts, often enough to cause a boater to stop and consider again before leaving a snug harbor.[18] It is a good thing that the Coast Guard still maintains this valuable link with our shared maritime past.

There was another federal shortcoming from the storm. The U.S. Revenue Marine Service (USRMS), with heritage from Alexander Hamilton's tax collecting fleet, was a valuable asset to exercise federal authority on the Great Lakes, especially along the international boundary. In 1913, the 145-foot U.S. Revenue Marine cutter *Morrill* "had the duty." A big part of the mission was "showing the flag," and in 1913, it was participating in the Perry Centennial and gathering water samples for the International Joint Commission. The centerpiece of the Perry Centennial was the U.S. Navy Brig *Niagara,* raised from underwater storage in Misery Bay. The *Niagara* was towed port to port by the USS *Michigan* with *Morrill* in attendance. But with the storm there was real work for her – gathering bodies of dead sailors and standing guard over the very dangerous floating hull of the *Charles Price*. Inexplicably a bureaucrat from the Washington office ordered her to Lake Erie to stand by the steamer *G.J. Grammer* aground at Lorain. The folks at the Lake Carriers' Association rightly fumed over the misuse of the *Morrill*. The *Grammer* was in no danger, but there was a critically important mission on Lake Huron that Washington was ignoring. It was a second black eye for Wilson and his team.

Reportedly some captains advocated for a federal law prohibiting ships from leaving port in defiance of a posted storm warning. To do so would be a criminal offense. Whether this was a serious recommendation or just a tale that a newspaper reporter picked up from an anonymous captain is unknown. My judgment is mostly hot air, a paper trying to stir the pot.[19]

The human cost of the storm is a different matter, especially as it related to financial payouts to the lost sailors. The Lake Carriers' Association's compensation to lost sailors' families was $18,245.60.[20] While we view this today as a pittance, it equaled roughly $429,543.81 in 2013 dollars. Assuming that each of 250 sailors equally shared in the pay out, it meant $72.98 in 1913 dollars or $1,718.17 a century later. By any standard, it was a very cheap value for a sailor's life, but historically sailors have never been valued highly.

The U.S. Revenue Cutter *Morrill* was taken off critical storm duty to "chase shadows" on Lake Erie.

The financial cost of the storm included $2,332,000 for vessels totally lost, $830,900 for vessels considered constructive total losses, $620,000 for vessels stranded but returned to service and approximately $1,000,000 in lost cargoes. Financial damage to coastal cities on the lakes isn't included.[21]

It is worth looking at the huge loss of shipping from a somewhat wider viewpoint. It can be argued that while the storm was especially violent, or perhaps the most powerful ever to strike the Great Lakes, a major reason so many vessels were lost was because there were so many on the lakes. The shippers were somewhat a victim of their own success and the booming North American economy. The greater demand for everything – grain, coal, ore, finished products – drove the need for more ships and provided a target rich environment when the weather monster struck.

Shipowners and captains are guilty for putting their ships and crews at risk, but the issue is, "Did they perceive the risk to be any greater than normal fall heavy weather sailing?" My conclusion is no. Yes, storm flags

The 1913 storm memorial at Goderich is especially stunning.
JOHN CHAREST

were up (or may have been dependent on what port they sailed from and when), but we expect storms in the fall. Through prudent navigation, hugging a shore, sheltering behind a headland or the like during the worst of it, we make our way through.

In this instance, the U.S. Weather Bureau was the villain. Not for failing to post the warnings, but for failing to adequately explain them. Had they put the hurricane signal up, the clear message of the severity of the storm would have been seen and better understood. A hurricane flag would not have kept all ships from sailing, but many would have found shelter until the worst passed. Forecasters on the lakes were literally "stabbed in the back" by the chair warmers in Washington who refused to allow the use of the hurricane signal. And good sailors died as the result.

Folks on the lakes never forgot the carnage of the 1913 hurricane. There were certainly other storms – the 1905 blow, the 1940 Armistice Day stem-winder, for example, as well as the gaggers that sunk the *Carl D. Bradley*, *Daniel J. Morrell* and *Edmund Fitzgerald*. But it was the 1913 hurricane that remained the prime example of how deadly Great Lake storms can be. On the 100th anniversary, many Great Lakes communities held memorials recognizing the terrible loss of life. Goderich, Ontario, on the lonely shore of Lake Huron, was especially active in erecting a stunning monument.

CHAPTER 8

What Happened

It is easy to conclude that the *Smith* sank in the storm, overwhelmed by wind and wave until she and her crew could no longer survive. The tough part is to determine *exactly* why she sank. What was the single item or, perchance, chain of failures that caused her to founder?

Even though the wreck has been finally found and efforts made to forensically evaluate her, there is no irrefutable smoking gun. This isn't unusual. Consider the *Edmund Fitzgerald* and the tremendous effort made (and to a point still being made) to determine her "proximate" cause of loss. Regardless of all the work, the best researchers can come up with is half a dozen "plausible" theories. There are others, such as alien abduction, that, although far-fetched, still have a devoted following. That said, some researchers will argue only that they know the "truth." Whatever. Beware of such zealots.

Material Issues – Brittle Steel/Hull Fracture

There is the theory the *Smith* could have broken in two on the surface, spilling much of her cargo before plummeting to the bottom of the lake. The fracture could have been purely driven by the stress of the storm or by "brittle" steel too weak to withstand the forces thrust on it.

From perhaps the beginning of steel ships through World War II, there were significant problems assuring adequate quality control of steel produced by the various steelmaking processes. For example, although the Bessemer process drove the price of steel down, which

The steel steamer *Western Reserve* broke in two in a moderate gale off Whitefish Point on August 30, 1892, with the loss of 26 of 27 aboard. She was running without cargo.

UNIVERSITY OF DETROIT/ MARINE HISTORICAL COLLECTION

helped feed the insatiable demand, it didn't necessarily improve quality. Everyone wanted steel, for the ever-expanding railroads, towering skyscrapers, bridges and other icons of the modern age. Ships, especially on the Great Lakes, took advantage of the inexpensive steel, too. Although never proven, it is thought that at least several vessels were lost when poor-quality Bessemer steel-hull plates fractured in a seaway. The 301-foot *Western Reserve* lost off Deer Park, Michigan, in Lake Superior on August 30, 1892, with 26 of 27 aboard is an excellent example. She was running light (empty of cargo) when she suddenly broke in two in a mild gale. There is speculation that her sister ship, the *W.R. Gilcher* lost off the Manitou Islands, Lake Michigan, on October 28, 1892, may have suffered the same fate, but no one survived to tell the tale. The quality of hull-plate steel continued to dog the maritime world to the extent that even the famous Liberty ships of World War II were prone to crack.[1] Recent material analysis work on the *Titanic* also suggests that her hull rivets were defective, thus contributing to the loss. Inferior steel certainly did make it into Great Lakes ships. In 1894, a naval architect, J.R. Oldham,

The 580-foot *Daniel J. Morrell* broke in two in a Lake Huron storm taking 28 of 29 men to the bottom.

stated to an international engineering session that some bad plates actually had to be cut out of ships after being incorporated into the hull.² It is not inconceivable that brittle steel could have ended up in a hull member with a resulting cataclysmic storm failure. However, there is no compelling evidence of it.

Working against the hull-break theory (non-brittle) is the argument that typically no Great Lakes ship ever breaks in two on the lakes while properly loaded and the *Smith* was carrying a full cargo of ore. There were no accusations that the *Smith* was improperly loaded, the ore not trimmed, too much forward, aft or midships. How a laker is loaded is very important and generally the first mate is charged with the responsibility of assuring it is done correctly. The two most famous broken ships on the Great Lakes, the 580-foot *Daniel J. Morrell* lost on Lake Huron on November 28, 1966, with 28 of 29 men, and 623-foot *Carl D. Bradley* on Lake Michigan on November 18, 1958, with 33 of 35 men, were both running empty.

According to the National Transportation Safety Board, the *Morrell* split due to the failure of the main hull girder amidships. The *Edward Y. Townsend*, sister ship to the *Morrell,* was about 20 miles distant and in the same weather conditions. She suffered structural fractures similar to the *Morrell*. The *Townsend* was declared a total

The 623-foot *Carl D. Bradley* broke in two in a Lake Michigan storm with the loss of 33 of 35 men aboard.

loss and laid up for two years following the storm. She later broke in two and sank in the North Atlantic while under tow to the scrap yard. The *Morrell* was built in West Bay City in 1906 and the *Bradley* in Lorain in 1927.

Anecdotally, a large number of lakers were sold for overseas scrapping when their useful lives were finished. Many, like the *Townsend*, didn't survive the trip, breaking and sinking in the Atlantic while under tow. Some were empty while others carried a load of scrap steel.

Ships properly laden with cargo are stronger than those running empty. Given this axiom and the fact the *Smith* was loaded with ore, breaking on the surface, while possible, isn't a likely scenario.

Construction Problems

It is easy to surmise that she may have been poorly built and that given the boom in construction and pressure to "build 'em and cut 'em," as well as periodic labor unrest in the shipyard, there were resulting deficiencies. This line of reasoning, however, doesn't hold up to scrutiny. Since the *Smith* was built in the American Ship Building Company's Lorain shipyard, let's look at the data for it. I selected 10 years worth of builds, four before the *Smith* in 1906 and five after 1906.

In 1902, nine lakers were built: four ran until the 1950s, three until the 1960s, one wrecked in 1940

141

A sistership of the Morrell, the *Edward Y. Townsend*, suffered a severe hull fracture in the same storm that sank her sister. She was also running light.

MARINE HISTORICAL SOCIETY

(*Sparta*, driven ashore at Pictured Rocks, Lake Superior) and one was lost by collision in 1910 (*Frank H. Goodyear*, rammed by *James B. Wood* above Pointe aux Barques, Lake Huron).

In 1903, eight lakers were built: five ran until the 1940s, one until the 1950s, two foundered in the 1913 storm (*Lewis Woodruff* as *Argus* and *R.E. Schuck* as *Hydrus*).

In 1904, three lakers were built: one ran until the 1940s, one until the 1950s and one until the 1960s.

In 1905, seven lakers were built: one ran until the 1950s, five ran until the 1960s, one until the 1970s.

In 1906, (the year the *Smith* was built), seven lakers were built: one ran until the 1950s, two until the 1960s, two into the 1970s, one (*D.R. Hanna*) sank from collision in 1919 (with the *Quincy A. Shaw* above Thunder Bay Light) and one (*Smith*) foundered in 1913.

In 1907, 10 lakers were built: one ran until the 1950s, four until the 1960s, three until the 1950s, one until the 1980s and one (*Cyprus*) foundered in 1907.

In 1908, seven lakers were built: one ran until the 1950s, five until the 1960s and one foundered in the 1913 storm (*John A. McGean*).

In 1909, seven lakers were built: two ran until the 1960s, one until the 1970s, three until the 1980s and one foundered in the 1913 storm (*Isaac M. Scott*).

In 1910, eight lakers were built: two ran until the 1960s, three until the 1970s, one until the 1980s, one sank in the Gulf of St. Lawrence under tow to the scrap yard (*Charles L. Hutchinson* as *Fayette Brown*) and one foundered in the 1913 storm (*Charles S. Price*).

In 1911, four lakers were built: one ran until the 1960s, two until the 1970s and one until the 1980s.

This is a reasonably good record. Various questions of design notwithstanding, the ships constructed in the American Ship Building Company Lorain yard stood the test of time. Of 70 ships built during this period, only seven foundered by storm, six of those in the 1913 screamer. Four others were lost by other causes: collision, blown ashore or sinking on the way to the scrapyard. But as a class, they ran successfully for a very long time, bucking storm, ice and other hazards of the trade until they finally wore out and were towed off for scrap.[3]

Peculiar Construction

J.R. Oldham, a well-known and respected Cleveland marine architect of the era, commented on typical ship type and construction. Oldham also was concerned with vessel hatches. "Lake steamers are of peculiar construction. They are about 18 times as long as they are deep, whereas the safe ratio of length to depth is 12 or 14 to one. The type won't be changed because it is the only sort of vessel that can navigate the lakes. The lake steamer must be able to carry a great cargo, but it must be shallow. So the type and general construction will remain the same. But the remedies I speak of will be made. They are practical and ship owners could adopt the changes if they would." We will hear from this learned man again.[4]

There was also speculation that the large number of hatches, 32 in total, resulted in a structural weakness in the *Smith*'s weather deck. Under the tremendous strain of the storm, the weak deck allowed the steamer to break in two. There is, however, little evidence to support this theory.[5]

Canadian naval architect W.E. Redway took a somewhat different view from Oldham. A member of the Institute of Naval Architects of England, he was one of the best known marine constructors on the Great Lakes and at the time was about the only member of the Institute of Naval Architecture in Canada, reflecting greatly on his expertise and experience.[6]

In a letter originally published in a Toronto newspaper, he focused on the theme that Great Lakes ships were built to a standard significantly lower than ocean vessels. Lloyd's of London rules required, for example, ship length not exceed 16 times hull depth. This was regularly ignored on the lakes, with many lakers 17 times or greater. Oldham earlier expostulated on the same premise. Redway explained his argument by pointing out that a laker and an ocean ship may have exactly the same weight of steel, but yet be different in strength. Taking it a bit further, if an ocean ship was a steel girder 4,750 tons in weight and 460 feet long, a laker girder of the same weight was 530 feet long. Based on the length-to-hull depth ratio, the ocean ship was much stronger. He also maintained that greater hull subdivision was needed. A typical laker only had three watertight bulkheads (those in the cargo hold were only "screen" bulkheads) in comparison to a similar ocean ship with six watertight bulkheads. They were telling arguments, but it always goes back to the balance of safety versus operational efficiency. The same argument was raised when the *Edmund Fitzgerald* sank on November 10, 1975, with the loss of all 29 hands. History does have this nasty habit of repeating itself. The safest thing is to leave the ship in the harbor, but once the decision is made to sail, operational efficiency rears its ugly but very necessary head.[7]

Naval architect W.E. Redway was the best known marine constructor in Canada.

Hatches

Many lakes marine men of the time felt that the *Smith* lost hatches and became waterlogged. While in the act of sinking, the thundering waves swept much of her upper works off, accounting for the amount and type of wreckage found east of Marquette. The testimony of the sailors from the *Denmark* and *Choctaw* concerning the unsecured hatches strengthens this explanation.

In point of fact, the only evidence that the hatches were not secured was from the *Denmark* and *Choctaw*. Did the whaleback crew see what they thought they saw? Or if the *Smith* crew was still working on the hatches, did they finish the job and do so properly, but after the *Choctaw* sailors stopped watching? An accusation isn't a fact.

Oldham stated, "The greatest fault with the lake steamers lies in their hatches. The hatch coamings are too low – about 12 inches in height. They should be 3 feet high. The hatches should be stronger and heavier and more attention paid to the hatch coverings."[8] Oldham's comments need to be taken with a great deal of gravity. He represented the United States at a variety of international naval architects conferences and delivered papers on Great Lakes vessels while attending.[9]

There is another hatch issue, perhaps best identified in the storm loss of the 420-foot, 4,900-ton steel steamer *Cyprus* off Lake Superior on October 11, 1907. Downbound from Superior, Wisconsin, with soft Mesabi Range iron ore, she fell off into the trough of the waves, cargo shifted and she rolled and sank. She was only 21 days old and on her second trip when she went down with 20 of 21 men. Seas were described by the lone survivor, Second Mate Charles Pitz, as "heavy" with a north-northwest wind. A little after noon, when the *Cyprus* passed the Pittsburgh steamer *George Stephenson* about 1,000 feet distant, her captain noted a long reddish wake coming from the *Cyprus*' ballast water discharge. Although she was riding the sea well, waves were boarding the weather deck. Otherwise, he thought she was doing well. About 6:45 p.m. the list had increased and when Pitz checked the hold, he noticed that the

The 420-foot steel steamer *Cyprus*.
THE MARINERS' MUSEUM

cargo had partially shifted and was mixing with water entering through the hatches. Mesabi ore is different from the hard ores of the old Marquette Range. Made up of fine grains, it runs freely and packs somewhat like sand. It is often red in color (thus the red wake), but also can be yellowish. Historically it was a stable cargo *unless* it became very wet. On this trip it was very, very wet. During this period, the soft Mesabi ores had a problem clogging the blast furnaces, so they were usually mixed with direct shipping ores, such as those from the Marquette Range.

Fifteen minutes after the cargo shift, the captain gathered the crew forward and had them put on life preservers and prepare the boats, but did not launch them. Half an hour later the *Cyprus* rolled portside over. They had waited too long. Crew, lifeboats and life raft all went tumbling into storm-tossed Lake Superior. For a few minutes there was shouting and desperate calls for help, then just the sound of the wind and waves.

The captain, first and second mates and a wheelsman ended up on a life raft drifting fast for the beach. The raft was stored forward and boats aft, so it was logical that the officers ended up on it. Four times the raft flipped over in the waves and four times the four men climbed back aboard. The fifth time it flipped, only Pitz managed to haul himself back on top. By now, though, he was a bare

The lone survivor of the *Cyprus*, Charles Pitz, made it ashore on the life raft.
MICHIGAN STATE ARCHIVES

300 feet offshore and in a few minutes was able to stand and fight his way to dry land. After a short time he was spotted by a surfman on beach patrol and taken to safety at the station. The Life-Savers started immediate patrols to try to find other survivors, but there were none, just the cold corpses of sailors. Eventually all but two of the bodies were recovered, a testament to the value of their life preservers in at least bringing the remains ashore.

Generally the loss of the *Cyprus* is blamed on the shifting cargo, but certainly other causes are possible such as a brittle-steel hull fracture around the turn of the bilge and thus out of sight of the crew.

Ominously the *Cyprus* was built in 1907, a year after the *Smith,* as hull No. 353 (the 10th laker after the *Smith*) in American Ship Building Company's Lorain yard. She was owned by the Lackawanna Steamship Company, a large operation at the time.

The common denominator between the *Cyprus* and *Smith,* beyond the builder, is the hatch closure system. Historic deck photos of both vessels lend strong evidence of the general commonality, as do underwater photos of both wrecks. If they were not identical systems, they were certainly variations on the theme. Both vessels had telescoping hatches, in effect steel leaves that slide under one another from the center of the hatch, outward to open and reversed to close much like a deck of cards.

When the decks are awash the value of watertight and secure hatches is apparent.

It appears that the system used was designed by Harry Brousseau, an engineer with the American Steel Barge Company in Duluth. A trusted engineer when the company was purchased in 1900 by the American Ship Building Company, he stepped up to superintendent of the engineering department. His original patent was filed in 1903 and others followed as he improved his design. His system called for 10 inverted U-shaped overlapping steel leaves per hatch, five opening to port and five to starboard. Each had a downward facing flange on the inboard edge that pushed against the adjacent leaf while opening. Leaves were pulled open or closed by a chain on each side. Ominously, perhaps, there is no mention in his patent of using tarpaulins or clamps on the hatches. It was anticipated that the leaves would "self-secure."

The chain motive power came via a long lineshaft assembled from various shorter sections coupled together and supported by a pillow-block bearing near each hatch. The shaft runs the length of the hatches, fore and aft. The chain is driven by a small sprocket on the shaft. When the shaft ran in one direction, the hatch opened. Reverse it and leaves slid closed. The three engines that drove the shaft, and thus the hatches, were spaced on the outboard starboard side of the weather deck.

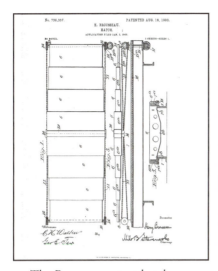 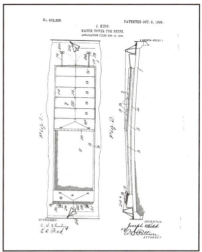

The Broussau patent hatch was not the only sliding hatch system on the market. Captain Joseph Kidd patented his "Hatch-Cover for Ships" on December 13, 1905. Kidd, of course, believed that his was the superior system, in part, as he maintained, because it would "provide a hatch which is practically water-tight or nearly so as possible when in place." It also called for a higher hatch coaming, from an estimated 6 inches on the *Cyprus* to a more robust 9 to 12 inches. The added size permitted more substantial clamps such as developed by Captain Mathew Mulholland.[10] For a while Kidd was the

(Top) Although of a somewhat different design to the system on the *Smith*, the *Cyprus* hatches were near identical. (Bottom) Hatch engines on the *Cyprus* were used to operate the telescoping hatches.

GREAT LAKES SHIPWRECK HISTORICAL SOCIETY

149

(Top) View of the *Cyprus* hatch engine with lateral chains and shafting visible.
GREAT LAKES SHIPWRECK HISTORICAL SOCIETY

(Bottom) Close-up of the *Smith* hatches and system.

superintendent of the American Steel Barge Company in Superior, Wisconsin, thus well aware of employee Brousseau's work.

Given that steel on steel is usually not considered a waterproof seal and the criticality of keeping water out of the cargo holds, it is reasonable to assume that the new telescoping hatches would have been covered with heavy tarpaulins, well secured in place, especially when storms were forecast. This would be a wrong assumption. The new *Cyprus* wasn't provided with tarps and it is believed that their lack directly caused the loss. Captain Kidd later stated, "no tarps were furnished to the *Cyprus*, the newfangled hatch covers were considered quite watertight and there was nothing on many of the new boats (to) which a tarpaulin could be attached."

The last part of Kidd's comment referred to the lack of hatch coaming height to mount clamps and room to install strongbacks and other securing gear.[11] Naval architect Oldham said much the same. Apparently the hatches themselves were intended to provide the security of a tight and strong closure without external supports.

Securing the hatches with tarps was vitally important. Great Lakes sailors knew well how their ships would "work" in a seaway, twisting and bending while driven by the force of the waves. Sometimes the action was powerful enough to spit rivets, sending them ricocheting across cargo holds like spent bullets. One captain reported

(Top) Note the rotating hatch shaft and lateral chain on the *Smith* hatch, also how weak the coaming is. (Bottom) The very low and insubstantial hatch coaming as well as opening/closing leaf chain is visible in the photo.
JERRY ELIASON

A slightly different view of a *Smith* hatch.
JERRY ELIASON

watching his telescoping hatches spring open when the waves pounded and twisted his ship, the action allowing massive amounts of water into the hold.[12]

The loss of the *Henry Steinbrenner* on May 11, 1953, offers some insight to the problem of telescoping hatch covers and tarpaulins, vessel design and captain decision-making. The 427-foot steamer was built by Jenks Shipbuilding Company in Port Huron in 1901.[13] In general design, she was very similar to the *Smith*, although a bit shorter and with 12 telescoping hatches instead of 31.[14] Her captain was Albert Stiglin from Vermilion, Ohio.

She was downbound on Lake Superior when a ripper storm overtook her, unleashing 75-mph winds and 20-foot waves.[15] As the storm intensified, a leaf on No. 11 worked loose, but was secured by the crew with great difficulty. The men had to hitch up to the traveling line running between the fore and aft houses to avoid being swept overboard. Like the *Smith,* she had no interior passageway.

As with the *Smith,* tarpaulins were not fitted over the hatches. As the storm progressed, the leaves opened, admitting more and more water into the cargo hold, more than the pumps could handle. The leaves were secured with Mulholland-style steel clamps, 28 per hatch.

At the height of the storm, the leaves on the stern-most hatches, Nos. 10, 11 and 12, worked loose and

Two leaves of a *Smith* hatch are still attached to the chain but clearly ripped off the hatch proper.
JERRY ELIASON

it was "Katy bar the door." The *Steinbrenner* was going down and fast. Seventeen of the 30 men aboard lost their lives, many due to difficulties with lifesaving gear and hypothermia.

The Coast Guard Board of Investigation concluded, "It was a general loosening of the clamps with the ship working in a heavy sea, metal to metal with metal clamps turned down on metal hatch covers, that aided the heavy seas in loosening the clamps. The seas swirling around the hatch coamings knocked over the loosened clamps." The board also stated, "The use of tarpaulins would have reduced the general loosening of the clamps and would have prevented free ingress of water between the hatch leaves."[16]

In connection with the decision not to use tarpaulins, the board concluded that "any reasonably prudent master could have used the same judgment under the same conditions with erroneous weather forecasts. … Failure to batten down the tarpaulins while under way and while conditions still permitted appears to be a situation where an experienced seaman underestimated the force of the sea."[17]

As the reviewing authority, the commandant of the Coast Guard disagreed with his investigation board. She wasn't lost to an "Act of God." Didn't the board conclude that if the tarpaulins were fitted, she wouldn't have sunk?

The *Willis B. Boyer*, now the museum ship *Col. James M. Schoonmaker* in Toledo, has one-piece hatches well secured with C-clamps.

Not fitting them was clearly the captain's responsibility and against Coast Guard regulations. "It should be the responsibility of the master to assure himself before leaving protected waters that all exposed cargo hatches of his vessel are closed and made properly tight." Failure to do so would contribute to the vessel's loss; therefore action was initiated against the master's license.[18]

As with the *Smith,* the hatch covers were the weak point, especially since they were not covered with tarpaulins. And like the *Smith,* the captain made a conscious decision not to fit them based on how he judged the weather, from experience and official forecast. Like Captain Owen 40 years prior, *Steinbrenner*'s Captain Stiglin made, in retrospect, a bad decision regarding whether to tarpaulin the hatches or not. Hindsight is, of course, 20/20.

The wreck of the *Henry Steinbrenner* has not been found. She reportedly sank 15 miles off Isle Royale Light. Whether the *Smith* routinely used either strongbacks or tarps is questionable. No photograph of her deck during her career shows either in place. Neither does the wreck video give any indication of tarps, clamps or strongbacks. The hatches were always closed on period photos and no

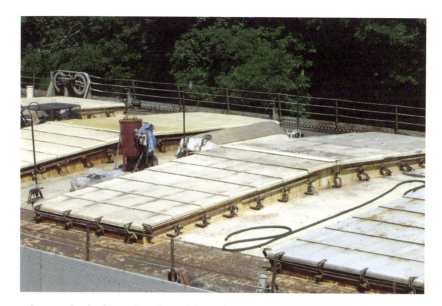

These leaf hatches on the steamer *Maumee* are secured by strong perimeter C-clamps, common practice today. No such clamps were on the *Smith* or *Cyprus*.

other method of securing them (clamps) or waterproofing them (tarps) was shown. This is not definitive proof, but it is very suggestive. The company trusted the hatches the way they were.

Captain Owen's fleetmate Captain C.D. Brown of the *Edwin F. Holmes* stated to his inquiry that the hatches were all properly battened down, but the canvas covers were not on. He was unable to explain why, since Captain Owen had used them previously. He believed that Captain Owen thought the weather was moderating and with seas falling off there would be no need for the extra labor of installing them. The only clear evidence that the *Smith* had canvas covers was Captain Brown's recollection.[19]

Prior to the advent of steel, hatch covers were simply made of wood in sections and covered with tarpaulins for water tightness when foul weather was anticipated. Properly secured, they were a good way of making hatches weather-tight. But as ships increased in size, wood hatches became impracticable. Opening and closing had to be done by hand, a time-consuming and labor-intensive activity. If not properly done up during heavy weather, the waves crashing on deck could force the

The older wooden hatches are clearly visible in this photo of a laker loading wheat in Duluth in the 1930s.

STEVE HAVERTY/GREAT LAKES STEAMSHIP SOCIETY

wooden covers off and subsequent waves flood the holds. Such wooden hatches were common to sea service, too.[20]

Captain James Kennedy of the steamer *Peter White* was upbound for Marquette on November 8, 1913, when he "struck some of the seas very heavily, causing the ship to vibrate so much that she broke quite a number of her wood hatch sections, which dropped into the hold." Given the severity of conditions, he anchored his ship in Grand Island Harbor on November 9. When his single anchor dragged in the hurricane wind, he put the second hook down. When he finally staggered into Marquette around noon on November 11, the steamer needed 41 new hatch sections.[21]

Engine Size and Horsepower

Naval architect J.R. Oldham argued, "For their size, Great Lakes vessels do not have enough power. With their shallow depth and extreme length they need a great deal of power to make headway against a wind. The average speed possible with the power they have now is nine knots. They should be able to make 12 knots. I don't know that even that would be enough."

The *Smith*'s triple expansion engine produced 1,700 horsepower, typical for the day but hardly considered especially powerful. By contrast the "super" class of lakers, such as the *A.H. Febert* built in 1942, were driven

156

by engines producing 4,400 horsepower at speeds of 15 mph. In all fairness, the new supers were 622 feet in length and 10,294 gross tons. The lower-power engines of the *Smith*'s era were economical, and they did the required job. That the ships lacked the power needed in extreme conditions is problematic. As technology steams forward, bigger and better ships are designed. This is called progress and it is simple second-guessing to apply later standards against earlier decisions. I will also add that in emergency conditions a ship can *never* have too much power!

Oldham continued, "The reason that I say lake steamers should have more power is that in those enclosed waters, they must be able to keep ahead in a wind. A matter of 10 miles out of its course and a steamer goes on the rocks. Unless it is powerful enough to drive onward, it is sure to be carried by the wind."[22]

Engine Failure

The coal-burning, hand-fired 1,700-horsepower triple expansion steam engine was common to those installed in many other era ships. It was comparatively simple and dependable. During World War II, all 2,700 Liberty ships built by the U.S. Government were powered by triple expansion steam engines. They were reliable and relatively simple to operate and repair. There is no reason to believe that an engine failure contributed to the *Smith*'s loss, although it easy to imagine the destruction of the ship if powerless in the midst of the storm.

Rudder

After her loss, one of the possible reasons mulled over by mariners was damage to her rudder. The idea was bolstered in 1976 when four Wisconsin divers discovered the wreck of the *Isaac M. Scott*, lost in Lake Huron in the same 1913 storm. Located upside down in 175 feet of water, an examination of the wreck showed the *Scott*'s rudder ripped loose from the ship. With the rudder so damaged, she would have stood no chance in the storm. Was the lost rudder the result of the wreck or the cause? Could the rudder on the *Smith* have failed, too, perhaps during the severe strain of the port turn to the Keweenaw? Or could the damage have been much later, closer to the location she sank? Without a completely functioning rudder, the captain's ability to keep a course into the seas would have been impossible. However, video appears to show the *Smith* rudder in place.

Spun Off Propeller

Although very rare, ships do occasionally "spin off" propellers. Minus a propeller, the ship is at the total mercy of wind and wave. Though very unlikely, it was considered possible at the time; however, video shows her propeller in place.

Lifeboats

Another mariner complained about the lifeboats. In a long newspaper interview, Mate Gordon Rattray of the Pickands Mather steamer *H.P. Hope* gave a candid appraisal that echoed testimony from Great Lakes sailors following every major loss, including the *Steinbrenner*, *Bradley*, *Morrell* and *Fitzgerald*. In general terms, it is still a problem for modern Great Lakes freighters.

"Great Lakes freight vessels carry two lifeboats and a raft, sometimes three and a liferaft. Each is supposed to carry 20 men. That is the usual size boat. They swing on davits high above the water.

"Not one of these Great Lakes lifeboats is made with ribs. They are made of some sort of plate about 1/16 inch thick, that bends easily – like a galvanized iron pail. They are uncovered boats – not decked over in any way. Even if they didn't roll over or fill in a sea, men in them would be exposed to the freezing weather that accompanies the storm that cost so many lives. These boats are meant to carry 20 men, are inspected by the U.S. Government inspectors and are supposed to be a means by which men may save their lives in a storm. And I defy anyone to take 15 men in one in a 40-mile breeze – that's moderate weather; the weather bureau would call it a brisk wind – and get anywhere in it. It would roll over and swamp.

"It would be impossible to lower one of these boats from the davits in a storm. One roll of the ship would smash the lifeboat as a tin pan when it was being lowered. The chances are one in a hundred against ever getting one of them into the water in a heavy gale." (Author's comment: This was nearly identical to testimony on the value of lifeboats given during the *Fitzgerald* investigation.)

"The loss of lives in the recent disastrous storm is an example of how much these boats amount to. As an experienced sailor, I declare that 75 percent of the lives lost might have been saved had the destroyed ships been equipped with lifeboats which could be lowered or which could be kept afloat and right side up after being lowered.

"Here's an illustration that might give point to my assertion that the lifeboats in use on the Great Lakes now are worse than useless. I was at one time second mate of the steamer *Superior City*. At Duluth I saw a U.S. inspector have a boat launched that on her inspection certificate called for 20 men. Nineteen men got into her. The captain was ordered by the inspector to make the 20 and the captain refused. The captain told the inspector to get in himself and the inspector wouldn't. While they were arguing up above, we were down in the boat, and I tell you I had to steady that boat at the side of the ship to keep from rolling over. There it was, one man shy of the number it was supposed to carry, about to roll over alongside the ore docks. I wouldn't have dared let it get away from the side of the ship. Finally, after neither the captain nor the inspector would get in, there being no one else on the ship, the boat was ordered back to the deck and that inspector okayed it.

"There should be a new type of boat on the Great Lakes. There should be a different way of getting it into the water. To my mind the ideal boat would be one of steel, 1/8- to 1/4-inch thick, bell- or cylinder-shaped and decked over with manholes to get into it, and equipped with covers and gaskets. Such a boat could be launched from a runway aft and shot clear into the water with the men in it – or it could be left on the ship, men could get

Captain Owen mastered the *Edwin F. Holmes* before bringing the *Henry B. Smith* out of the shipyard in 1906.

into it and when the ship turned over or went down, the lifeboat would float off."

Does this remind the reader of a lifeboat on a modern ocean freighter? Mounted high on the stern on a set of rails, the boat is ready to be launched into the sea as needed. Rattray was 50 years ahead of his time.[23]

"The fault lies with the U.S. government. If the inspectors would refuse to okay the useless boats now, there would have to be a change in the model of the lifeboats and in the method of leaving a crippled ship. By instructions of the printed rules of our managers and under the U.S. inspection laws, these lifeboats are kept in as perfect condition as possible all through the sailing season. I don't blame the lake carriers or ship owners. I blame the government."[24]

Human Failure, Pressure on Captain Owen

How much pressure the owners may have placed on Captain Owen is questionable. Just after the loss one anonymous mariner stated, "This is, of course, a delicate question and I would not want to be quoted on it. Naturally the owners want dispatch, but they don't want more dispatch than is consistent with safety. I can't help but believe that the loss of the *Smith* is due primarily to a fatal error in judgment. The storm could not have been underestimated. The Weather Bureaus were still giving the most alarming warnings. The strength and seaworthiness of the *Smith* must therefore have been overestimated. It's a serious thing even to have to think of allotting the blame for such a terrible disaster."25

Captain C.D. Brown, master of the laker *Edwin F. Holmes* of the Acme Transit Company (Hawgoods), took vehement exception to the charges that Captain Owen was under pressure from the Hawgoods. Captain Brown and his ship were in Marquette to load ore when he spoke with a local reporter. Acme Transit was managed by the Hawgoods and the *Holmes* was Captain Owen's previous command. He stated, "The story is absurd and a great injustice to the Hawgoods. It has no basis in fact and there can be no foundation for it but irresponsible gossip. The suggestion that Captain Owen's actions were in any way ... (obscured text) is ridiculous. It is unfair to Captain Owen's memory and to the managers of the line.

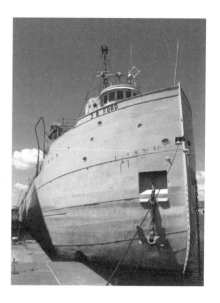

The bow of the *J.B. Ford*. Note the added bow thruster.
STEVE HAVERTY/GREAT LAKES STEAMSHIP SOCIETY

"Captain Owen was one of the oldest masters working for the line and has been 30 years in employ. He was a seasoned sailor, a man of 58 years, accustomed to important command and regarded as a fine sailor. He was perhaps the best master in the fleet and was esteemed as such by the Hawgoods. They had every confidence in his ability and his judgment. I cannot for a moment believe he had any orders conflicting with the general orders to the line's masters to handle their ships to gain the greatest dispatch consistent with safety."

Captain Brown had been sailing for the company for 10 years. A news reporter questioned if he ever had any orders to push his ship in unsettled weather or been reprimanded for holding in port when the lake was rough or storms threatened. Captain Brown looked the scribe in the eye and stated he never had any "orders but to handle my boat safely. And I never have been reprimanded for any delays I have encountered either in the season's work or because I waited for settled weather. The Hawgoods

(Left) Part of the original machinery space in the *Holmes* (the *J.B. Ford* today). (Right) The *J.B. Ford* still has her original turret style pilothouse, a near twin to the *Smith*'s.

STEVE HAVERTY/GREAT LAKES STEAMSHIP SOCIETY

are both former active sailors and they are reasonable men."

The Hawgoods may have been "reasonable men," as Captain Brown said, but the charges of forcing Captain Owen to sail into the storm stung deeply. In fact, it was reported from Cleveland that the company would be filing a suit for civil libel against the *Marquette Chronicle* for promulgating the baseless charges. The Hawgoods stated, "The charge is false in every particular and in every intendment and in every insinuation. We have retained counsel to bring action civilly and if the statutes of Michigan permit, we will proceed criminally against the author of the article."

The managers were incensed by comments like, "Captain Owen was under a threat. This explains why he left port in the teeth of a storm. He was told to make time. He had a run of hard luck and was eager to please his employers." Also, "'Bring your ship through on time.' Such was the order given the commander of the *Smith* and Captain Owen, like all good seamen, obeyed his orders for it is said luck in running the boat on schedule this season broke bad for the captain and experienced navigator, as … his ship frequently was overdue and

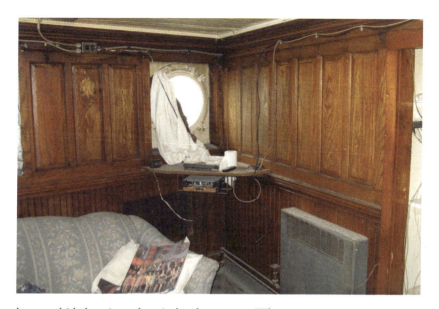

Decorative woodwork on the *Holmes* would have been similar to that of the *Smith*.

STEVE HAVERTY/GREAT LAKES STEAMSHIP SOCIETY

he was chided again and again by the owners. When he cleared Cleveland on the fatal voyage, it is said he had orders to run on schedule time at any cost and that failure to comply with the owners' demands might mean the loss of his commission."[26]

There were other supposed statements by Captain Owen that were of questionable veracity such as, "I will clear as soon as the ore is aboard" and "Wire the company that I am coming," both uttered while the "storm raged outside the breakwater." As he was backing away from the dock, the fearless reporter claimed he said, "I will go down lake with the wind and make up lost time." The article ended with, "The price of his company's folly was the *Henry B. Smith*, a loyal captain and 30 lives."[27]

All this hoopla aside, I can find no record of an actual lawsuit being filed. Doubtless the Hawgoods wanted to quickly defuse a volatile charge as quickly as they could. And certainly once the *Marquette Chronicle* filed the salacious story, it was hard for other papers not to repeat it. By contrast the *Daily Mining Journal* (Marquette) played the *Smith* disaster "down the middle" without making incendiary charges.

Henry A. Hawgood was another of the Hawgood fleet damaged in the storm.

The *Daily Mining Journal* (Marquette) was the big gun in the city. Old and established, it was the newspaper of choice for most folks. By contrast the *Marquette Chronicle* was a short-lived affair that was eventually absorbed by the *Mining Journal* in 1919. In 1913, the *Chronicle* was by far the "edgier" newspaper, seeking to scoop the *Mining Journal* whenever possible. It also appears to have a more pro-labor bent. Given the temper of the times, with labor unrest sparking throughout the industrial areas of the country, including the Michigan iron and copper ranges, and shipyards painting the "greedy" vessel owners as villains living off the slave labor of their crews, it is understandable. Add to it the 250 or so sailors killed in the storm and the *Chronicle* was just stirring the pot of public opinion. The general thrust of the story was in turn picked up by other Great Lakes newspapers.

The storm had not been kind to the Hawgoods: the *Smith* lost with all hands, *Henry A. Hawgood* on the beach near Fort Gratiot and the *J.M. Jenks* ashore in Georgian Bay. The *Jenks* was initially thought to be a total loss, but in end was barely salvageable. While the *Hawgood* and *Jenks* could be considered "normal" although expensive accidents, the loss of the *Smith* was entirely another matter. While they weren't alone in facing such a catastrophe, it didn't make it any easier.

In my opinion, the whole issue of the captain being under undue pressure from the owners was created by period newspapers looking for a good angle to the tragic story. Captain Owen was a trusted master who brought two new builds out of the shipyard for the company and continued on in the *Smith* for the last seven years. If he didn't consistently run her to the owners' satisfaction, he would have been fired long before. The pressure charge doesn't pass the smell test, but it is a good juicy story, so the papers ran with it. Are we any different today?

Illustrating how seriously the issue of not recklessly endangering a vessel and crew was taken, reportedly one major shipping company required a general policy statement hung in every wheelhouse stating, in part, "Bring your vessel home safe."²⁸ To suggest that Great Lakes captains were a bunch of irresponsible men willing to sail dead into storms without regard to the lives of their men or vessels is ludicrous.

The *J.M. Jenks* as the *Ralph S. Caulkins* (1941-1963).

All captains face a degree of pressure from vessel owners and operators to manage costs, avoid accidents and keep to schedule. As stressed again and again, ships don't earn money by waiting in port to load or discharge cargo, by anchoring every time the lake gets "misty" or sheltering when it gets "wavy."

As a point of macabre coincidence, Captain Owen had previously sailed for a time on the steamer *Iosco*, thereby seeing service on two of the lake's "went missing" ships. The *Iosco*, and her barge *Olive Jeanette*, disappeared with all hands near the Huron Islands west of Marquette in a September 1905 storm. It is interesting that the *Smith* sank so relatively close to her, perhaps only 30 miles to the northeast. Considering the size of the Great Lakes, 95,000 square miles, it is remarkable coincidence.

Captain Brown of the *Holmes* also went with landlooker Dan Johnson, who discovered much steamer

Captain Owen previously sailed on the *Iosco*, another of Lake Superior's still missing wrecks.

wreckage east of the city, and verified that while some was from the *Smith*, wreckage from the *Waldo* was also present. Captain Brown was also well familiar with the *Waldo*. Other than the obvious marked items, he was certain the cabin doors were from the *Smith*. A brass lock on a piece of one was the type used by the American Ship Building Company and *Smith* came out of the Lorain yard.

Message in a Bottle

On or about December 1, the first message in a bottle (in this case a pint flask) was found, purportedly from the *Smith*. The small rolled-up paper, likely torn from a pocket notebook, was discovered by Dan Johnson while searching the coast near 20 miles east of Munising. Supposedly it said, "If found forward to the folks at home, address E.D. Carter, care of Porter Marine Post Office, Detroit, Michigan. We ... ," and then it unexpectedly stopped. There was no Carter among the crew. Was it real or a hoax?[29]

The mystery of why the *Smith* sunk was further confused in June 1914 when another message in a bottle was found by a fisherman at Mamaimse Point on the north shore, 35 miles from Whitefish Point. Dated

November 12, the note as printed in the *Daily Mining Journal* (Marquette) read: "Dear Sir: Steamer *H.B. Smith* broke at the number five hatch. We are not able to save her. (Line missing.) Had one hard time on Superior. Went down 12 miles east of Marquette. Please give this message to owners." The signature was not legible. Torn and faded, the entire message was difficult to read.[30] As typical with such messages, it resolved nothing.

There is also a question on whether it was found in a bottle or the ship's message tube. Brass message tubes were often used on steamers of this era. Kept in the wheelhouse, it was intended that they would contain the last crew list and be thrown overboard if it looked like the ship was lost. They were rarely actually used, but it was a great idea.

After much debate, the *Smith*'s owners concluded (at least publicly) that the message was a fake. The major reason was the discrepancy in dates. Since it was dated November 12, while the *Smith* left Marquette on the 9th and actually sank late that night or early the next day, the timing was clearly wrong. Did the shipboard writer confuse the dates in the stress of the sinking or was the shore side hoaxer so misinformed as to make such an obvious error? The final bullet in the hoax was the given location, 12 miles east of Marquette. It is clearly very far from the wreck's actual location.

As expected, there was reportedly at least one other "message in a bottle" from the *Smith*. It was dismissed out of hand as a disreputable hoax, kind of an early version of making false radio distress calls today.

Shoaling

After the wreck, there was some speculation that she may have come too close to Granite Island and struck an outlying shoal. Thus damaged, she plunged to the bottom either immediately or later as the damaged hull eventually broke up. This same argument is made with the *Fitzgerald,* striking Caribou Shoal, though with considerably more likelihood and evidence. Granite Island is about 11 miles north of Marquette and generally on the track the *Smith* could have taken to the Keweenaw. There is, however, no evidence to support this theory. There is no outlying shoal and while the light on Granite was doubtless dimmed by the snow and storm, it was functioning and would have warned the steamer clear. Captain Owen was also very familiar with the area and would have steered well clear on his run to the Keweenaw.

In the Final Analysis

So what does the evidence show? What actually sank the *Henry B. Smith*? Unfortunately, there is no smoking gun, no irrefutable proof establishing the cause of loss within a "reasonable doubt."

Invariably, though, shipwrecks are caused by a cascade of events, one thing leading to another until the final one breaks the camel's back. But let's consider two of the most probable causes of loss.

Location of Wreck

The approximate area of foundering is 36 miles SSE of Keweenaw Point, a little less than 30 miles from Marquette. It rests in approximately 535 feet of water. A lack of bodies would tend to indicate that the sinking was rapid and most of the crew trapped within. The finding of the cook's body wasn't considered significant, since local marine men felt cooks were usually the first in a crew to don life jackets. (Is this just a little stereotypical?) It suggests that the cook, recovered in his life belt, as well as an engineer, later found on Goulais Point in the eastern lake, were simply swept overboard during the height of the storm rather than part of an organized attempt to abandon ship.

Surface Break

Sonar imagery and video imagery shows the wreck essentially sitting in a field of iron. The amount of ore is unknown but is certainly a significant amount. The *Smith* appears to be "broken" around mid-deck. The forward half is somewhat bow high. The stern deckhouse

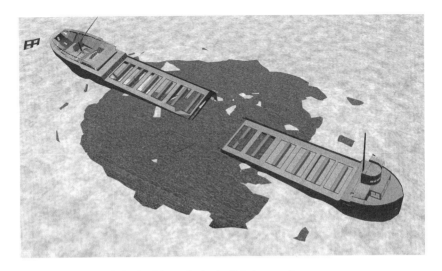

(Illustration) The *Smith* is sitting on top of a large field of spilled iron ore.
JERRY ELIASON

is generally demolished, although the hull is intact. It is possible that the aft deckhouse damage is the result of the explosion of one or both boilers when the cold lake water hit them as she was heading for the bottom. Such explosions on sinking ships were not uncommon. It could also be argued that the powerful boarding seas were the cause of the destruction. The boiler explosion can only be absolutely determined by perhaps snaking a small remotely operated vehicle down through the wreckage and into the engine room, a most remarkable if not impossible feat. A third alternative is water pressure simply crushing the deckhouse down to the deck, leaving the jumbled rubble seen today.

A likely scenario for the break is that she was proceeding on course for the shelter of the Keweenaw and suffered a catastrophic hull fracture, causing part of the ore to spill out her bottom, raining to the lake floor with the ship quickly following, landing roughly atop the cargo. This theory follows both Oldham's and Redway's general comments. So far so good.

But several factors work against the surface break theory.

There are no examples of ore-loaded lakers breaking in two during storms (I can't find a single instance). In fact, the heavy ore serves to "stiffen" the hull of the ship, making it less likely to fracture. The hull of a ship can be compared to an eggshell. Filled with yolk and white, the shell is much stronger than just shell alone.

The *Smith* was a relatively new ship, so corroded hull plates/girders were not likely present. The fracturing of both the *Carl D. Bradley* and *Daniel J. Morrell* can be traced to much older vessels with hull maintenance issues.

A surface break is also made unlikely by how close together the two sections are, virtually touching. Complete surface fractures invariably result in the two sections being widely separated, perhaps by hundreds of feet, as each part reacts differently to the action of wind, wave and buoyancy. The deeper the water, the greater the distance.

The upper wheelhouse engine room telegraph is in "full ahead." Given that she was bound for the Keweenaw and a bit underpowered, would the captain have driven her at full speed through the storm or checked her back to half speed to lessen stress on the ship? The telegraph position would therefore seem to indicate that she was in a more desperate condition, but more on that later. It also reinforces the idea of a cataclysmic loss, a "right now" event.

The second engineer and second cook were both wearing life preservers. This is unusual on a few levels. First, unless the ship is in extremis, crewmen invariably do not don life preservers. This implies that the breakup was slow enough to allow the time to find and put on preservers. If the engineer was in the engine room, there likely wasn't time to get topside. Whether the cook was on duty or off, time to don a jacket was very limited. Whatever happened gave enough warning for at least these two men to don preservers. Perhaps others did, too. Some bodies likely slipped out of the preservers, sinking eternally to Lake Superior's icy bottom. The common life preserver of the period did not have a strap running between the legs to keep the user from slipping out. Other bodies could have washed ashore only to be lost forever on the desolate coast.

The engine room telegraph on the upper helm is still in the "full ahead" position.
JERRY ELIASON

Capsize

A second theory is that the *Smith* fell off into the trough of the waves, rolled onto her beam ends, the ore cargo tumbled, blowing out her weak hatches and raining to the bottom. The ship hung for a bit before taking the final roll, allowing some crew enough time to don life jackets. If the ore wasn't properly trimmed, the likelihood was greater. It was (and still is) important that the ore be leveled across the hold, not left with a pile in the middle when it tumbled from the chutes. Leaving it in a hump increased the chance of a cargo shift. There is no evidence that the *Smith* cargo was properly trimmed, but I would surmise it was, as it was common practice for the dock crew to routinely do so. To have *not* done it would have been extraordinary.

Naval architect Oldham weighed in, "Cargoes of these vessels always should be trimmed. Ore or coal, when loaded into the ships, should be leveled off. Restated a little differently, it should never be allowed to remain in a hump as delivered by the chute. There is no doubt in my mind but that several of the vessels lost in this storm went on their beam ends in the gale because their cargoes shifted. Shifting of a cargo of ore, coal or grain will send a steamer over on its side at once."[31]

It is worth considering whether the *Smith* trimmed the ore or not after loading. Given the press of time, could Captain Owen have skipped this important step, thus rendering the ship more prone to capsizing? That said, there is no evidence that he did not properly trim his cargo.

Oldham continued, "Once on beam ends, water would pour in through the loosely covered low hatches and the steamer will capsize or sink."[32] Beam ends means the ship is listing so far over her beam as to be nearly perpendicular. Her righting power is gone, so she will not roll back upright. The desperate condition is invariably the result of a shifting cargo and invariably leads to her loss.

As with anyone speaking against the prevailing order of things, Oldham's recommendations were generally sloughed off by vessel owners. But certainly his description of shifting cargo and a ship on her beam ends could have accurately described the end of the *Smith*.

How and why a ship capsizes, or alternatively remains upright, is important to understand. Not to wander too deep into technical issues, but it goes back to the idea that the weight of a ship can be thought of as a single force acting through a single point (aka the center of gravity) and the buoyancy of the water is another single force acting through another single point (aka the center of buoyancy). The center of buoyancy is the point which would have been the center of gravity of the water the ship displaced. With rarest of exceptions, the center of gravity is almost always above the center of buoyancy.

Ships like the 1913 lakers were single-hulled ships designed to float vertically with the center of gravity and center of buoyancy on the centerline. If the ship lists to one side, but the center of buoyancy doesn't change, the weight and balance acts such as to make the ship want to list further until she finally rolls over and capsizes (aka "beam ends").

Normally, as a ship lists the center of buoyancy shifts, causing one of four actions to occur.

1. The ship reaches a position in which the centers of gravity and buoyancy are in a vertical line (one directly above the other). This gives the ship a more or less

permanent list. Often this happens as the result of a ship taking on water, which in turn has migrated to one side, or shifting cargo.[33]

2. She may list until the top of one side of the hull is underwater (capsizing). At this point the ship usually will sink.

3. The ship could continue right over, sometimes called "turning turtle." If enough air is trapped inside the hull, she could float for a considerable period of time. The *Charles Price* in Lake Huron is an example of this outcome.

4. If well designed, the ship will act to return to the upright position, the center of buoyancy shifting to cause this positive outcome. Should the center of buoyancy move too far in the other direction, the ship will follow, causing her to roll, and the effect continues in alternating directions.[34]

There can also be an issue with fore and aft motion of a ship known as pitching. Again, it is caused by a moving center of gravity. Bucking into heavy seas certainly increases the effect dramatically, especially as ships are far longer than they are wide. For a 1913 laker, it can easily be an 18-to-1 ratio.

A ship, of course, isn't a solid object, but rather a thin shell of steel with internal bracing. Pitching heavily in high seas can introduce significant stresses on the hull, sometimes severe enough to break her in two. Height of waves, distance between crests, cargo stowage and hull strength all play a major role in determining whether the ship lives or dies, as evidenced by the *Bradley*, *Morrell* and others.

Although not germane directly to the *Smith*, it is worth understanding that the problem of stability in iron ore carriers is perhaps a more serious issue today than a century ago. Instead of the old direct shipping ore of years gone by and the current pellets, common on the Great Lakes at present, much of the world market is in "fines," a general term indicating the physical form of a mineral or similar cargo, namely a large proportion of small particles. Shipping iron ore fines by sea from the

Indian subcontinent has become problematic in recent years if moisture content has been too high when loaded. As a result, the supposedly solid cargo behaves as a liquid, often with alarming results.

Technically this phenomenon is called liquefaction and causes severe stability problems by allowing the cargo to shift at sea. The best outcome is a severe list. The worst is capsizing. Much of the problem is traced to the monsoon season (June to September), since the fines are stored outside, usually without any protection from heavy rain. For example, in 2007 the bulker *Asian Forest* capsized and in 2009 *Black Rose* did the same trick. Both losses were traced to the liquefaction of the iron ore fines.

Naval architects Oldham and Redway both spoke to the problem of a lack of engine power, especially as it related to being caught off a lee shore in a storm. Without sufficient power to battle wind and wave, period lakers were certain to wreck by being driven ashore. If lucky it was a "forgiving" sand beach. If unlucky it was ship-killing rock. If a U.S. Life-Saving Service crew was available, the crew would likely survive as with the *L.C. Waldo*. If not, they often didn't. Sailing was still a dangerous business.

What wasn't discussed involved falling off into the deep trough of storm waves. Once in the deadly trough, lakers often didn't have the power to drive out. The rudder had to be hard over and engine "full ahead" at just the right instant to make the turn and force the vessel up and back into the seas. It was a difficult maneuver for a captain to make and very dependent on perfect timing and enough engine power to "kick her around" in a down-wave cycle. If the seas were too big, it was impossible. Caught in the trough, the ship would roll to unholy angles, causing the cargo to shift to the lee side, throwing her over on her beam ends, ending in disaster.

In both the capsizing and breaking scenarios, the hatches played a critical role. The telescoping hatches on the *Smith* were neither watertight nor strong enough to resist the pounding of the seas sweeping over her deck in the 1913 storm. Massive quantities of water flooded into the hold, especially when the bending and flexing of the hull opened significant gaps between leaves. The water had two critical negative effects. The added weight forced the steamer deeper into the lake, constantly decreasing her freeboard and making her more susceptible to wave damage and flooding. As the water increased in the holds, she became less responsive to the helm and more sluggish. As her bow drove into the seas, it gradually rose less and less. Finally, to an extent the water was "free," thus when she rolled it rushed to the low side, increasing the list and driving the tendency to fall on her beam ends. It is possible to postulate that the incredible hull stress fractured the steamer, sending her to the bottom to land atop much of her spilled ore cargo. It was all over in mere minutes. Incidentally, while every hatch was not examined by the camera, every hatch examined was found to be open, giving the appearance of leaves being forced off.

Sisters in Disaster:
Cyprus, Henry B. Smith* and *Henry Steinbrenner

The best clues to what happened to the *Smith* are found in the *Cyprus* and *Henry Steinbrenner*. In my view the three are intrinsically linked.

1. Both the *Cyprus* and *Smith* were built in the Lorain yard of American Ship Building Company, the *Cyprus* in 1907, *Smith* in 1906. The *Steinbrenner* was a Jenkins build in 1901.

2. All were essentially the same design, the *Cyprus* 420 feet, *Steinbrenner* at 427 feet and the *Smith* 525 feet. While a difference of 105 feet (*Cyprus* and *Smith*) may seem large, in reality it made little difference. Remember American Ship Building and the comment about "built them by the mile and cut 'em off wherever the owner wanted." The same construction methods and techniques, fitting and gear was used in all the boats sliding out of the booming shipyard. Any owner's individual requirements, such as observation deck forward, special fittings in the owner's suite and so forth, had no real effect on the vessel.

The steamship *Henry Steinbrenner* also had telescoping hatches.

3. All were considered well built and sturdy. The *Cyprus* was as "seaworthy a vessel as has ever been turned out by a lake shipyard," *The Marine Review*, a Cleveland trade publication, said after the sinking. The *Steinbrenner* just passed her five-year survey prior to loss. After the loss of the *Smith*, *Beeson's Marine*, another trade publication, called her "a staunch vessel." Following the losses, there were no negative comments found regarding any vessel.

4. The vital hatch cover system, if not identical, was very close in design. It would be hard to find any significant differences between them. Remember that the lone survivor of the *Cyprus* sinking reported large amounts of water in the cargo hold from leaking hatch leaves. The *Steinbrenner*'s system was somewhat different but similar enough to be a fair representation.

5. The issue of tarpaulin covers (tarps) for the hatches was critical to the three ships.

a. The *Cyprus* didn't cover her hatches with tarps on her final trip because none were given to the ship. She was apparently expected to run without using them. Both the *Smith* and *Steinbrenner* had the canvas covers, but their captains decided against their use.

b. By witness, in the instance of the *Cyprus* and *Steinbrenner*, not covering the hatches with tarps allowed a large amount of water to enter the cargo hold, resulting in a list, eventual capsize and a dive for the bottom.

c. According to Captain C.D. Brown of the *Edwin F. Holmes*, Captain Owen's fleet mate, the *Smith* had tarps for the hatches. Strangely, none of the literature of

The *Henry Steinbrenner* had added cross-hatch fasteners. They proved inadequate.

the 1913 storm or *Smith* disaster mentions tarps, only "hatch covers." The two are distinctly different parts of a complementary system.

    d. No witness to the *Smith* departing Marquette mentioned seeing tarps installed or being installed. The only comment was from sailors on the *Denmark* and *Choctaw* to the effect that the men were still securing the hatches as she pulled round the breakwater. This has traditionally been taken to mean working on closing the telescoping hatch covers. This is likely in error. Putting on tarps is slow and laborious work and would be obvious to any observer, especially a ship master or crewman. Whether to use them or not is traditionally the judgment of the master. If Captain Owen believed the storm was dying off as evidenced by the weather recordings, he certainly had every reason to anticipate falling seas and winds throughout the night. In 16 hours, give or take, he could be in the St. Marys River system, so why waste the time putting on the tarps he really didn't need? The underwater video shows no indication of tarps or securing strongbacks for them. Without contradictory evidence, I conclude the tarps were not installed.

    6. In the case of the *Cyprus,* she sank because the company hadn't provided tarps for the hatches. In that

of the *Smith,* she had tarps but, fooled by the weather, Captain Owen decided not to use them. Had he installed the tarps, in my opinion he would have survived. Captain Stiglin made the same error with the *Steinbrenner.*

7. While many have expressed less than dramatic concern over the hatch problem, the editors of the *Coast Seamen's Journal; a Journal of Seamen, by Seamen, For Seamen* did so.[35] The editors claimed that after the loss of the *Cyprus,* the U.S. Steamboat Inspection Service in Duluth ordered better hatch fasteners to be used. Ship owners protested to Washington and the supervising inspector general overruled his Duluth office.

8. There is a macabre link between the *Cyprus*, *Smith* and *L.C. Waldo* (wrecked on Keweenaw Point). The last laker to see the *Cyprus* afloat was the *George Stephenson*, the same vessel that spotted the *Waldo* on Gull Rock. And if we stretch the realm of "maybe" just a little, *Stephenson* was in the area when the *Smith* dove for the bottom.

9. Although certainly pure coincidence, the *Cyprus*, like the *Smith*, was discovered by shipwreck hunters on the 100th anniversary year of loss. In August 2007, a team from the Great Lakes Shipwreck Historical Society working from the RV *David Boyd* discovered her in 460 feet of water. Largely intact, she is mute testimony to the problems of telescoping hatches. The *Steinbrenner* remains undiscovered.

My 10 Cents Worth

After considering the various theoretical possibilities, examining the historical aspects of Great Lakes shipwrecks and viewing the available video of the wreck, this is my working conclusion. I say "working" because it may well modify if/when additional video documentation is produced. Remember that historians, mariners and just plain folks are still arguing over what sunk the *Edmund Fitzgerald,* so I have no doubt questions on the *Smith* will continue for the foreseeable future.

1. Once she left Marquette, Captain Owen realized he couldn't continue to Sault Ste. Marie on his current course with wind and sea abeam, so he turned to port

The 440-foot *Denmark* was also weather-bound in Marquette Harbor.

to shelter under the Keweenaw. In theory, every mile he made to the northwest brought him into increasingly calmer sea conditions.

   a. His hatches were not fully closed when he left Marquette, as evidenced by the sailors on the *Denmark* and *Choctaw*. The work was finished fairly quickly, however, so when he hit the big seas, they were as secure as they could be.

   b. The very design of the hatches (steel on steel, low coaming, no strongbacks) is immaterial at this point. He was soon taking on water through the hatch covers just as the *Cyprus* and *Steinbrenner* had.

   c. He did not have the canvas covers (tarps) in place over the hatches. This would have made them far more watertight, but installing them is a slow and laborious process. This decision was not made to save time as much as it was the result of his perception the weather was moderating, so why go through the work of adding them? Regardless, they were only another layer of protection; the telescoping hatches should be good enough on their own to withstand the occasional boarding sea. Remember, he was expecting moderating wind and seas, not increasing.

d. The *Smith* was not the only laker in port. The other vessels, including the 440-foot *Denmark,* built in 1909, and *Choctaw,* were older, smaller and less seaworthy than the *Smith.* They weren't going anywhere until the lake moderated considerably. Their crews took time to gawk at the big laker.

2. After he began to encounter significant weather, Captain Owen's only course of action was to continue on for the shelter of the Keweenaw. He couldn't return to Marquette. The Lower Harbor is small and constrained by docks, a breakwater, rocks and other hazards. He could put the *Smith* right on the beach, just "full ahead" until he found bottom, but he doubtless believed that it was better to stay offshore regardless of the storm than to willfully cast his ship away. Since man began sailing, it's been a decision captains had to make. Most opted for sea rather than shore.

3. Waves continued to sweep the deck, grasping and smashing into the hatches. As the hours passed, wave size increased.

4. As time progressed more and more water flooded into the cargo hold via the hatches. Some was expelled by pumps, but much wasn't. The twisting and turning of the hull forced gaps to appear in the steel hatch covers, each an entryway for water.

5. The extra weight of the water coming aboard forced the *Smith* deeper into the water, decreasing her freeboard and increasing the susceptibility to the waves sweeping the deck, resulting in more water flooding into the hold and possibly dismounting hatch leaves, too. Remember, the steel lip in coaming and hatch leaves was weak.

6. As the ship becomes increasingly sluggish one of two things happens:

a. The free water in the hold causes her to roll severely (either port or starboard) and fall on her beam ends, going over completely or nearly so. The heavy iron ore smashes out through a number of hatches raining to the bottom. Water gushes into the hold via the now completely open hatches and the *Smith* plummets to the bottom, breaking in two either on impact or during the wrecking action, ending up on top of the spilled ore.

    OR

    b. The free water in her hold adds so much stress to the hull that it fractures and the *Smith* drops to the bottom, resting on top of the part of her cargo that poured out of the fracture point.

    c. In either case, air in the cargo hold that didn't already escape in the previous scenarios now blows off hatch covers as the ship settles to the bottom. The complete status of all hatch covers is unknown. Most appear off with hatches yawning open. The only exception are the two hatches immediately aft of the forward deckhouse.

    7. The sterncastle damage was caused either by direct storm action, literally being knocked apart by the waves, crushed by the depths or a boiler explosion when the cold water hit the red-hot boiler. I tend to believe a boiler explosion.

    8. The crew were dead men from the time they left Marquette. Given the weather and extreme difficulty of putting a lifeboat in the water and strong hypothermia conditions, Captain Owen either put the ship on the beach or all was lost. And there wasn't any beach once he turned for the Keweenaw, just desolate shore and unforgiving rock. That the two bodies recovered wore life preservers is some evidence that there was knowledge that the ship was in extremis. The lack of other bodies indicates that Captain Owen never ordered "abandon ship," resulting in the crew at large donning preservers. Contrast the few bodies recovered from the *Smith* (two verified) versus the large number from the Lake Huron losses, some of which were catastrophic (abandon ship right now!) and others with enough time to launch a lifeboat.

    9. The loss of the *Smith* was the result of error in judgment by Captain Owen. There was no inordinate pressure from the owners to "bring her in on time or be fired" or similar comment. He simply misread the weather that he could see and with no significantly better

data from the Weather Bureau sailed off into the "sucker hole." His telescoping steel hatches were closed, but not tarped over, and entering into "moderating weather" he didn't judge it necessary. And there, but for the grace of God, could have gone so many other good ships and crews under the same circumstances.

In the End

Like the *Edmund Fitzgerald* there were no survivors and no witnesses. And the wreckage itself doesn't provide a smoking gun, just lots of smoke. Perhaps after a great deal more exploration that missing gun will be found … but I doubt it. So you make the call! For me the *Henry B. Smith* is found … but remains a continuing mystery of the Big Lake.

The Future

The *Henry B. Smith* wreck will attract more and more attention, resulting in increasing exploration and photo/video documentation. The analysis of the new material may well reveal what really caused the ship to founder. What in fact was the proverbial straw that broke the camel's back?

CHAPTER 9

Mystery Solved

The *Henry B. Smith* was found on May 24, 2013, by a small team of dedicated shipwreck hunters. It made national, even international, news. She had been missing almost a century, but through decades of effort, the shipwreck hunters put it all together and solved one of the biggest mysteries of the Inland Seas.

Most Great Lakes shipwreck divers are content to explore known wrecks, to photograph them and probe for their hidden secrets. In their heart of hearts though, all dream of finding a "virgin wreck," an undiscovered wreck never before found. Rarely do their dreams come true. Searching for such wrecks is hard work, requires fairly expensive technology and is very time consuming. There are also no guarantees of success. But there are divers who raise their game and accomplish the near impossible task of finding virgin wrecks. The group that found the *Henry B. Smith* is extraordinary in that not only did they find her, but many others, too, either individually or as part of a team. In part, the *Smith* is their story.

Lake Superior was calm that morning as the small outboard slowly churned through the water. Aboard were three of the most successful shipwreck hunters on the Great Lakes: Jerry Eliason, Ken Merryman and Kraig Smith. The friends have sought undiscovered shipwrecks for many years, one media outlet calling the trio the "Great Lakes legendary shipwreck hunters." Eliason works as a regional supervisor at the Minnesota Department of Public Safety, Smith as a CFO (chief financial officer) to a company manufacturing weighing equipment. Merryman is a computer design engineer, but in his spare time runs a charter service on his boat *Heyboy*.[1]

Suddenly things became very exciting, very fast! Eliason later related, "For me those couple minutes we were seeing the *Henry B. Smith* flying bridge live was an 'all the hours of shipwreck hunting, research and money spent was worth it' realization. When I saw that flying bridge video live, I was making sounds that convinced Ken that I somehow had hidden a woman on the boat and was having sex with her!"

All of the team members on the boat that day had a single overwhelming common denominator – the powerful desire to solve the mysteries of the lost ships of the Great Lakes. In addition, they were very experienced wreck divers.

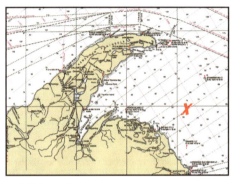

The location of the long-lost shipwreck *Henry B. Smith*.

Eliason started diving in 1966 at the age of 13, first hitting Lake Superior two years later. By 1976, he was wreck diving on a regular basis; typically about 50 wreck dives a year. He and Smith met on Isle Royale in 1979 while both were diving with different groups. Merryman joined the pair in 1992.

The team's shipwreck-finding activities started in 1999 when Eliason's son, Jarrod, working with his father, built their first effective side-scan sonar system. Things really came together later in the year when Smith purchased his C-Dory, a trailerable fiberglass cuddy cabin skiff. It was a perfect search platform for sensitive electronics like side-scan sonar and video cameras.

Other than the consuming desire to find undiscovered shipwrecks, team members bring critical skills and experience to the table.

Besides being a computer engineer by trade, Merryman is a confirmed wreck diver. From the early 1970s, he was running dive charters to Isle Royale, the Apostle Islands and the Minnesota North Shore. In 1977,

Ken Merryman, Jerry Eliason and Kraig Smith.
JERRY ELIASON

he led the group that discovered the *Kamloops*, lost off Isle Royale in a December 1927 storm, and in 1991 discovered the tug *T.H. Camp* in the Apostles. However, perhaps his greatest accomplishment is his work in the formation of the Great Lakes Shipwreck Preservation Society (GLSPS) in 1995. It is the leader in the diving community, answering the question, "OK, you found it. Now what do you do?" Part of the GLSPS answer is to place wrecks on the National Register of Historic Places.

Smith admits that he participates "simply for the adventure … the excitement of solving a mystery. It's not TV, but a great experience. What we are going to find next, what is just out of sight, realizing most likely no one else has ever seen this before. Friendship is No. 1, then pursuit, leaning forward with a shared objective to apply thought, conversation and energy toward."

The objective of all the work was always in clear focus. Eliason said it's like "winning the Stanley Cup. We have our private celebration first, and then right away we start thinking about going to find the next one."

Smith relates, "It takes a lot of perseverance, that's for sure," noting the team went through a dry spell of 14 years without finding one of several shipwrecks they were seeking. "We were really grinding for quite a while."

The group is well respected. Brendon Baillod, a noted maritime historian, said, "There are only about 50 serious shipwreck hunters on the whole Great Lakes and those guys on western Lake Superior are in the top five."

With all due respect, I rate them clearly as No. 1 on the Big Lake.

The team never specifically went after the *Smith*. Rather they went to Big Bay in late May 2013 to evaluate several geologic anomalies discovered by sifting through a huge amount of geologic data. This is a tale in itself. One of the group's long-term projects was to find the *U-656* off Cape Race, Newfoundland.[2] To this end, Eliason wrote to a plethora of federal agencies using the Freedom of Information Act (FOIA) requesting information on how they cataloged static anomalies off the East Coast. As Eliason later said, "So when we were out hunting for German submarines, we wouldn't get all excited that we had a German sub when in reality all we had was a geologic anomaly in the same place all the time (presumably a shipwreck)."

In response to his FOIA requests, he received a series of replies in effect saying, "We don't have what you want but check with this other agency." Some replies came from rather obscure agencies including the National Geospatial Intelligence Agency.

Eliason related, "Ultimately last November (2012), I received a letter providing me with access and instructions on what they had, with the notation that the data they were providing access to wouldn't do me any good in finding shipwrecks, but here it is. I was amazed and surprised to find that not only was there a treasure trove of geologic data for the East Coast, but also the Great Lakes. In raw form, the data was just millions and millions of numbers, which is where my wife came in. She is a wiz at processing and graphing data. The raw data didn't say, 'Here's a possible wreck,' but between my wife, son and me, we developed some data processing formulas." (Author's note: Karen is a remarkably talented software engineer.)

Since Eliason knew where most of the known wrecks in Lake Superior are located, the group used the process on available data to focus on several known wrecks.

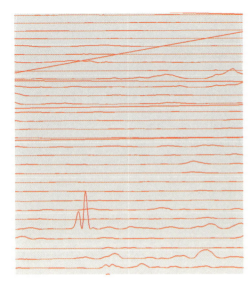

After manipulating and filtering the data, this spike proved to be the elusive *Smith*.

JERRY ELIASON

The first wreck to jump off the bottom after processing and graphing the data was the *Superior City*.[3] Proving the fragility of the data, other wrecks like the *Cowle*[4] and *Edmund Fitzgerald*[5] did not stand out. But since the *Superior City* proved the analysis methodology, they applied the process in other sections of the lake. One of the data analysis anomalies turned out to be the *Henry B. Smith*. Another of the data analysis anomalies was the *Cyprus*.[6] Proving the variability of the data, three other targets turned out to be geology. Oddly, another target wasn't a shipwreck ... or at least yet. Apparently it was a surface ship swept up when the original data was collected. This is, of course, a very cursory explanation of the process used. There are still a number of potential targets to evaluate and widely distributing the exact methods would be counterproductive.

Eliason describes finding the *Smith* thusly, "When we headed out, the weather was good, but not great or perfect. I wasn't sure we weren't just going for a long boat ride. I was driving the boat and as we slowed down, just before hitting the waypoint selected by placing the curser on my wife's graph of the area, I saw what looked like fish about 120 feet above the bottom. I now know the fish-finder was picking up the bow mast, but I couldn't imagine it could be that easy, so we launched the side-scan and started a pass from a point half a mile north and east of the waypoint. When we got to the west end of the selected one-mile pass, we dropped south 0.1 nautical mile and saw the huge anomaly partly caused by the wreck and partly caused by the rain of iron ore. There were strong geometric acoustic shadows that suggested we had something more than geology. We then launched

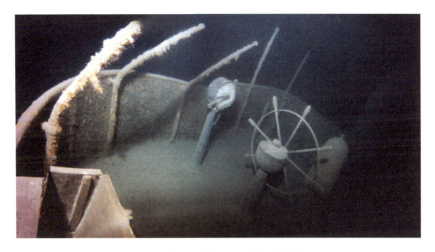

the camera (drop camera) and started seeing disturbed bottom like we commonly see around wrecks. She teased us for a while, but while moving the camera we winded up seeing a steel pole (forward mast) that said this was a manmade anomaly, not a natural one. Ken, Kraig and I have been fortunate to have been through this several times before, but when we got the camera on the pilot house and flying bridge, I knew it was the best find of my career. The *Benjamin Noble* had a lot of allure, but turned out to be not a very good wreck. The *Judge Hart* was and is a superbly intact wreck, but lacking on the history and other intangibles. The *Henry B. Smith* has it all – history, mystery and a beautiful wreck."

(Top) The upper helm is a spectacular image. The telegraph is still set for "full ahead."
(Bottom) The steel pole clearly indicated the team had found a wreck.
JERRY ELIASON

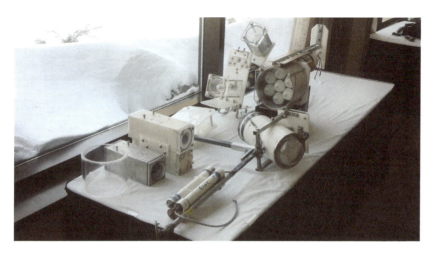

All search gear was designed and built in-house.

The sonar Eliason mentioned was obviously key to finding the wreck. Rather than use an off-the-shelf commercial model, however, the team was using one largely built and designed by his son, Jarrod. Why do things the easy way, just plunking down a pile of money and deploying a state-of-the-art super magnetron, hyper flux capacitor, Sonar-Matic when you can make your own? Of course, this plan only works if you have a brilliant engineer as a son. A magna cum laude graduate of Kettering University and the primary inventor of nine U.S. patents and a contributor to nine more, Jarrod found his father's shipwreck projects to be a nice change of pace. Although not physically on the boat that fateful day, his spirit certainly was there. The critical sonar wasn't the result of an afternoon's tinkering in the shop, but rather the product of years of thought, trial and error and testing. In fact, roughly 22 years worth of effort and countless models, variations and permutations, each building on previous success and adding more capability and performance. And behind each one was Jarrod's work.

This reinforces the unique nature of this shipwreck hunting team. Just throwing money at a search wasn't their method. Rather, focusing on the goal and structuring the tools needed to accomplish it was far better. And they validate their method with success again and again.

Perhaps there is a little magic in Smith's boat, too. Six of the eight virgin wrecks the group located since 2004 have been from the C-Dory. Dan Fountain, another experienced diver and wreck hunter, joined the team the second day to help muscle the camera and its heavy cable.[7]

Eliason reminisced, "The biggest problem with exploring the *Henry B. Smith* is that the most photogenic section of the wreck – the bow – is also the most dangerous. Because it is so perfectly intact, including all

(Top) A spare propeller blade is secured aft.
(Bottom) Wooden frames in the lower wheelhouse are still intact.
JERRY ELIASON

the rigging, the chance of snagging the camera is high. I currently have one camera (permanently fouled) on the *Olive Jeanette* and another on the *Moonlight*.[8] It's just a matter of time before we end up with a camera on the bow if we continue exploring the bow without the perfect wind." Since the camera is a drop device, it "flies" with the movement of the boat, thus wind and resulting drift are critical.

This list of heretofore undiscovered or forgotten wrecks located by the team is most impressive. And remember it does not include others' original finds, like of the *A.A. Parker*,[9] *Olive Jeanette* and *Cyprus*. They only went after those ships because it was irritating that someone else had the numbers (latitude and longitude) and they didn't.

1977 – *Kamloops*, 250-foot package freighter bound from Montreal for Fort William that "went missing" in a tremendous storm on December 1, 1927, with all 22

(Top) There is no doubt the wreck is the *Henry B. Smith*.
JERRY ELIASON

(Bottom) Canada Steamship Lines' *Kamloops*.
PUBLIC ARCHIVES OF CANADA

The *Theano* yielded to new technology.
KEN E.THRO COLLECTION

hands. Ken Merryman led a group that discovered her on the west side of Isle Royale.

1981 – *Theano* (propeller only), 255-foot three-island steel package freighter owned by Algoma Central Railway, lost November 17, 1906, with a cargo of steel rails, east off Trowbridge Island, Ontario, east of Thunder Cape. During the height of the storm, she struck Marvin Island, smashing a hole in the hull and sinking. All of her crew escaped in her boats.

1982 – *William C. Moreland*, 580-foot bulk freighter, lost October 18, 1910, on Sawtooth Reef off Eagle River, Michigan. It was only her fifth trip when she "found" Sawtooth while blinded by smoke from forest fires. The bow later broke off, sinking in deep water. Her stern was salvaged in 1911 and joined to a new bow, the ship emerging from the yard as the *Sir Trevor Dawson*.

1988 – *Onoko*, 287-foot bulk freighter, lost September 15, 1915, off Knife Island, Minnesota. Built by the Globe Iron Works in Cleveland, she was the first iron-hulled freighter on the Great Lakes and the largest vessel on the lakes. Regardless of her ground-breaking attributes, she was considered by marine men to be "the worst looking sight on our inland seas," "far from

(Top) The *William C. Moreland* hard up on Sawtooth Reef. Note her broken hull. (Bottom) Down she goes. The *Onoko* dives for the bottom of Lake Superior.
KEN E. THRO COLLECTION

beautiful" and "an eyesore." After springing a hull plate under her engine room, she slowly dove for the bottom. It is thought that she either damaged her hull in an earlier grounding incident or suffered injury during a storm a few days before. All crew escaped.

1990 – *Judge Hart*, 253-foot steel bulk freighter, lost November 28, 1942, in Ashburton Bay, Ontario, with a grain cargo. She was downbound when, as the result of a navigation error, she punched into a boulder hard enough to hold her in place. After initial assessments showed her not much damaged, she was hauled off only to quickly fill and sink. All crew escaped.

The *Benjamin Noble* in Duluth.
KEN E. THRO COLLECTION

2004 – *Thomas Friant*, 96-foot fish tug, lost January 6, 1924, 13 miles SSE of Two Harbors, Minnesota. She was carrying a group of fishermen when her hull was cut by ice. All passengers and crew escaped. She also was occasionally used as a tug and excursion boat.

2004 – *Moonlight*, 206-foot schooner-barge, lost on September 13, 1903, off Michigan Island, Apostle Islands. She was under tow of the steamer *Volunteer* when the hawser broke in a stem-winding gale. Luckily, the steamer was able to take the crew off before she foundered.

2004 – *Benjamin Noble* (aka *Benj. Noble*), lost in a storm April 27, 1914, between Two Harbors and Duluth, Minnesota. All 22 crew went down with her. Reportedly overloaded, she carried a very heavy cargo of steel rails. As the story goes, she tried to enter Duluth during the storm but one of the twin breakwater lights was out and rather than chance it, turned back into the storm-whipped lake, sailing into legend. Her wooden pilothouse later washed up on Minnesota Point.

2005 – The *Judge Hart* (entire ship). See previous page for details.

2005 – *Marquette*, 235-foot wood bulk freighter, lost October 15, 1903, near the Apostle Islands, Wisconsin. She was downbound with iron ore in fair seas when she suddenly sprang a leak, sinking bow first. All crew

At 850 feet down, the *Scotiadoc* is the deepest wreck discovered in the Great Lakes.

escaped in her lifeboats. Coincidently, she was the sixth vessel owned by the Gilchrist Transportation Company to be lost in 1903.

2010 – *Ontario*, 297-foot steel barge, lost October 13, 1927, east of Outer Island in the Apostle Islands. She was under tow of the tug *Butterfield* when she "found bottom."

2013 – *Henry B. Smith*, previously listed, see Chapter 8.

2013 – *Scotiadoc*, 416-foot bulk freighter, lost after a collision in heavy fog with the steamer *Burlington* off Thunder Bay, Ontario, on June 21, 1953. One of her crew of 29 was killed when a lifeboat being lowered overturned. She was downbound for Georgian Bay with wheat. At 850 feet, she is considered the deepest shipwreck in the Great Lakes known discovered.

By any standard this is a most impressive list of successes, like finding a needle in a haystack again and again. In a way their achievement borders on the mystic, but in reality it is the result of huge amounts of hard work, brilliant engineering and experience.

For me it is time for a toast to their triumphs past and for those yet to come!

Endnotes

Chapter 1

[1] A magnetic anomaly in geophysics is an irregularity in magnetic strength on the earth's surface. While usually caused by differences in the magnetization of the rocks it can also be indicative of steel shipwrecks or, in the case of iron ore, cargo.

[2] U.S. Navy Fact File P-3 Orion, http://www.navy.mil/navydata/fact_display.asp?cid=1100&tid=1400&ct=1

[3] Welcome to the USS *Defender*, http://www.defender.navy.mil/default.aspx.

Chapter 2

[1] aka "muscle power," an expression meaning manpower or hard, physical labor. It likely first appeared in nautical slang before being picked up into general use and refers to the characteristically impressive strength of Norwegian sailors.

[2] *Blue Book of American Shipping*, 1907, Cleveland, 1907, 398.

[3] Hulett Iron Ore Unloaders, https://www.asme.org/getmedia/59a21de6-56b6-4da8-a4d8-520b74c3e86e/199-Hulett-Ore-Unloaders.aspx.

[4] Hulett Iron Ore Unloaders, op. cit.

[5] The self-unloader has, of course, greatly increased the speed and versatility of unloading lakers.

[6] The idea of "building them by the mile and just cutting off whatever size was wanted" didn't originate in the Great Lakes. The same joke was prevalent in England in the 1850s and before, when the huge number of merchant service sailing vessels were identical in nearly every way.

[7] Bruce W. Bowlus, *Iron Ore Transport on the Great Lakes: The Development of a Delivery System to Feed American Industry*. (McFarlane and Company, New York), 125-127, 176-177.

[8] *Pacific Marine Review*, Volume 16, 1919, 104.

[9] aka "spar" deck.

[10] American Lloyds, *Record of American and Foreign Ships – 1907*, American Bureau of Shipping, New York.

[11] John O. Greenwood, *The Fleet Histories, Volume Six*, (Cleveland: Freshwater Press, 1995), 181.

[12] aka wheelhouse, pilothouse and bridge.

[13] Newspaper Clipping, unidentified, undated.

[14] Profile and Deck Plans, *H.B. Smith*.

[15] *History of Bay County, Michigan* - H.R. Page, 1883; *History of Bay County – Bay City illustrated*. (Bay City, Mich.), Board of trade, C.&J. Gregory Company, n.d.); J.O. Greenwood, *Fleet Histories, Volume 6*, (Cleveland: Freshwater Press, 1998), 181; Ron Bloomfield, *Legendary Locals of Bay City*, (Charleston, SC: Arcadia Press, n.d.), 173-174.

[16] *Ludington Daily News*, April 18, 1906; Perry F. Powers, *History of Northern Michigan and Its People Volume 3*, (Chicago: Lewis Publishing Co., 1912), 1166; *The Disston Crucible, a Magazine for the Millmen*, Vol. 3-4, February 1914, 141.

[17] *Ludington Daily News*, November 3, 1983; Email, Paul W. Schopp to author, June 8, 1997.

[18] John O. Greenwood. *The Fleet Histories, Volume Six* (Cleveland: Freshwater Press, 1998), 147-153.

[19] *Duluth News Tribune*, August 16, 1906.

[20] *Duluth News Tribune*, June 6, 2013.

[21] *Duluth Herald*, November 15, 1913.

[22] *Star Beacon*, July 8, 2012.

[23] Incredibly the *Ford* still exists, although the breakers torch is hovering over her. Her classic lines remain unchanged and the old turret-style wheelhouse is original. Her engine room contains a vast collection of authentic machinery including the old triple expansion steam engine. Realizing her historic importance, the Great Lakes Steamship Society worked hard to save her for future generations, but it was an impossible task. Unable to raise the money needed, she is doomed to the scrapyard of history.

[24] Steamship *J.B. Ford*, http://www.shipjbfordhistoricalsurvey.com/.

[25] Kathleen Pletsch, *Centennial Tribute to the Victims of the Storm*, (Goderich, Ontario: Great Lakes Storm Remembrance Committee, 2013) 119.

[26] Scotch Boiler, http://en.wikipedia.org/wiki/Scotch_marine_boiler.

CHAPTER 3

[1] Perfectly Deadly - http://news.nationalgeographic.com/news/2000/06/0609_hurricane.html.

[2] *Annual Report*, Lake Carriers' Association, 1914.

[3] NOAA Two Weather Systems Collide, http://www.regions.noaa.gov/great-lakes/centennial_anniversary_storm_of_1913/storm-meteorology-2/.

[4] "The 'White Hurricane' Storm of November 1913, A Numerical Model Retrospective," Richard Wagenmaker NWS Detroit; Dr. Greg Mann NWS Detroit, http://www.crh.noaa.gov/images/dtx/climate/1913Retrospective.pdf.

[5] "The 'White Hurricane' Storm of November 1913, A Numerical Model Retrospective" op. cit.

[6] Including relief light vessels.

⁷Gustav Kobbe, "Life on the South Shore Lightship," *Century Magazine*, August 1891.

⁸*Annual Report, U.S. Life-Saving Service*, 1914, 91-92.

⁹*Port Huron Times-Herald*, November 12, 1913.

¹⁰*Annual Report US Life-Saving Service*, 1914, p. 92-93.

Chapter 4

¹*Owen Sound Sun*, May 27, 1913; *The Shipbuilder*, October 1913; "The Large Canadian Steamer *James Carruthers*," *Marine Engineering Log*, Volume 19, 201-208.

²*Telescope*, November 1963, 247-253; *U.S. Merchant Vessels List* 1914; *U.S. Merchant Vessels List* 1913.

³*Marquette Chronicle*, November 16, 1913.

⁴The number of passengers and crew vary with the source.

⁵*Port Huron Times-Herald*, November 12, 1913.

⁶*Annual Report U.S. Life-Saving Service*, 1914, 90-91.

⁷*Marquette Chronicle*, November 15, 1913.

⁸*Annual Report U.S. Life-Saving Service*, 1914, p. 93.

⁹*Port Huron Times-Herald*, November 11, 1913; Edward Kanaby, survivor of the 1913 Storm on the Great Lakes, https://www.youtube.com/watch?v=NG4UGmrOLVg.

¹⁰*Annual Report U.S. Life-Saving Service*, 1914, 91.

¹¹These were ship's lifeboats, not the specially designed and built "lifeboats" used by the U.S. Life-Saving Service.

¹²This was likely the big steamer *Matthew Anderson* aground.

¹³*Port Huron Times-Herald*, November 11, 1913.

¹⁴"We have met the enemy and he is us." Pogo

Chapter 5

¹In 1913, Fort William and Port Arthur were individual cities. They were later combined into today's Thunder Bay.

²Beeson, Harvey C., *Beeson's Inland Marine Directory, 1913*.

³*Daily Mining Journal* (Marquette), November 21, 1913.

⁴In old charts Ile Parisienne was called Parisian Island.

⁵Some stories have confused her location to Sand Island in the Apostles, making the "Sandy" Island in Whitefish Bay into "Sand" Island.

⁶*Daily Mining Journal* (Marquette), November 15, 1913.

⁷A sounding machine is a contemporary form of depth finder, automatically lowering a weighted line to the bottom and retrieving while indicating depth.

⁸Cat's Paw – a locking device for an anchor chain; chock – a steel/iron casing which serves as a lead for lines or chain; Wildcat – the portion on the end of the windlass that handles the chain or lines, a chainwheel.

[9] Letter, Captain Noble of the steamer *Cornell* to Mr. A.F. Harvey, assistant general manager, Pittsburgh Steamship Company, n.d.

[10] *Daily Mining Journal* (Marquette), November 15, 1913.

[11] *Daily Mining Journal* (Marquette), November 12, 1913.

[12] A submarine bell was usually lowered over the side of a lightship and operated by compressed air. In the case of Whitefish Point, it was mounted on a tripod-like device and controlled from shore. The striking of the bell could be heard for long distances by a "listen man" stationed under the waterline in the forepeak of a ship. The bell was a relatively new aid for Great Lakes mariners, only established on August 15, 1912. It was 2,187 yards north of the point in 180 feet of water. A sparbuoy was over it to keep ships from fouling the cable that actuated the bell. It was replaced by a submarine oscillator, which had a greater range, on June 6, 1925.

[13] Letter, Captain F.B. Selee of the steamer *Alexander McDougall* to Mr. A.F. Harvey, assistant general manager, Pittsburgh Steamship Company, n.d.

[14] During this period, lunch was called dinner. The evening meal was known as supper.

[15] Letter, Captain West of the steamer *William G. Mather* to Mr. A.F. Harvey, assistant general manager, Pittsburgh Steamship Company, n.d.

[16] *Daily Mining Journal* (Marquette), November 10, 1913.

Chapter 6

[1] Porthole to landlubbers.

[2] *Marquette Chronicle*, November 11, 1913; the lifeboat comment is at odds with Captain Mosher's report.

[3] Mosher later recorded the cost of the sleigh and fisherman at $13.

[4] "The 'White Hurricane' Storm of November 1913, A Numerical Model Retrospective" op. cit.

[5] Keweenaw County Historical Society, KCHS papers. n.d.

[6] *Daily Mining Gazette* (Houghton), November 11, 1913.

[7] C. Fred Rydholm, *Superior Heartland, Volume II*, (Marquette, Michigan: Privately published by C. Fred Rydholm, 1989), 1045.

[8] *Marquette Chronicle*, November 15, 1913.

[9] The *Choctaw* had her own relationship with the *Waldo*. On May 20, 1896, the *Waldo* rammed and sunk the whaleback in the St. Marys River.

[10] Logbook, U.S. Life-Saving Station at Marquette, Michigan, November 9, 1913.

[11] All U.S. Life-Saving Service surfmen were rated from 1 to 8, with 1 being the most skillful and experienced and 8 the least. In the event that the keeper was absent, the No. 1 man took over for him.

[12] The correct number on each boat is impossible to determine. Some USLSS records differ from personal accounts of participants.

[13] *Cornell Daily Sun*, December 6, 1913.

Chapter 7

[1] *Daily Mining Journal* (Marquette), November 13, 1913.

[2] *Daily Mining Journal* (Marquette), November 17, 1913.

[3] *Daily Mining Journal* (Marquette), November 15, 1913.

[4] *Daily Mining Journal* (Marquette), November 16, 1913.

[5] *Daily Mining Journal* (Marquette), November 20, 1913; the wreckage has since "gone missing."

[6] Some evidence suggests the number was 27, but there is room for error up and down. The official "Wreck Report" lists 26 names.

[7] *Daily Mining Journal* (Marquette), November 24, 1913.

[8] *Daily Mining Journal* (Marquette), November 18, 1913.

[9] *Marquette Chronicle*, November 21, 1913.

[10] *Daily Mining Journal* (Marquette), November 20, 1913.

[11] *Daily Mining Journal* (Marquette), November 16, 1913.

[12] *Marquette Chronicle*, November 17, 1913.

[13] *Evening News* (Sault Ste. Marie, Michigan), November 22, 1913.

[14] SNAFU – Situation Normal, All Fouled Up

[15] Letter, Captain W.T. Mooney, Steamer *Andaste*.

[16] *Cleveland Plain Dealer*, November 15, 1913.

[17] *Marquette Chronicle*, November 17, 1913.

[18] U.S. Coast Guard, Storm Flags, http://www.uscg.mil/news/stormcenter/

[19] *Marquette Chronicle*, November 22, 1913.

[20] David G. Brown, *White Hurricane : A Great Lakes November Gale and America's Deadliest Maritime Disaster,* (International Marine Publishing: New York), 236.

[21] *1913 Lake Carriers Annual Report*, 1914.

Chapter 8

[1] Different sources give different numbers of Liberties suffering brittle steel fractures. The American Welding Society https://www.aws.org/about/blockbuster.html claims that eight (of the 2,710 built) were lost due to brittle steel, placing the cause of fracturing as steels that were notch sensitive at operating temperatures. The steel was found to have high sulfur and phosphorus contents. However Liberty Ship Problems, http://en.wikipedia.org/wiki/Liberty_ship#Problems, states that there were nearly 1,500 claimed instances of significant brittle fractures. Research showed that ships in the North Atlantic were exposed to temperatures that could fall below a critical point when the mechanism of failure changed from ductile to brittle, therefore allowing the hull to fracture rather easily.

[2] Bruce W. Bowlus, op. cit., 150.

[3] American Ship Building – Lorain, http://www.shipbuildinghistory.com/history/shipyards/2large/inactive/amshiplorain.htm

[4] *Daily Mining Journal* (Marquette), November 15, 1913.

[5] *Daily Mining Journal* (Marquette), November 16, 1913.

[6] *The Globe* (Toronto), January 1, 1898.

[7] *Duluth Herald*, December 1, 1913.

[8] Hatch coamings today are higher and far stronger than those on the *Smith* and period ships.

[9] *Transactions of the Royal Institution of Naval Architects Volume 39*, American Society of Naval Architects and Marine Engineers, 1897, xivii; *Journal of the Society of Naval Engineers*, Delivered Paper "Steamers of the Great Lakes as Regards Strength," Washington, D.C., 1894.

[10] Captain Mathew Mulholland established the Mulholland Fastener Company specializing in the design of hatch cover clamps and related equipment for retrofit and new construction, many incorporating tarpaulin systems. The company never designed or constructed complete hatches.

[11] A strongback is a bar placed across a hatch to lock it in position. Typically several were used for each hatch.

[12] The *Cyprus* History, http://www.boatnerd.com/pictures/historic/Cyprus/Part13-14.htm.

[13] Jenks Shipbuilding Company, http://www.shipbuildinghistory.com/history/shipyards/719thcentury/Jenks.htm.

[14] On 24-foot centers.

[15] This is technically "hurricane force," but the U.S. Weather Bureau didn't call them that in 1953 either.

[16] Marine Board of Investigation, Foundering of SS *Henry Steinbrenner* Off Passage Island, Lake Superior, May 11, 1953, with loss of life.

[17] Marine Board, op. cit.

[18] Marine Board, op. cit.

[19] *Daily Mining Journal* (Marquette), November 17, 1913.

[20] Wooden hatches were not infallible. Many of those from the *L.C. Waldo* were torn off by the seas, ending up ashore from Big Bay Point to Marquette.

[21] Letter Captain James Kennedy. Steamer "*Peter White*."

[22] *Daily Mining Journal* (Marquette), November 15, 1913.

[23] Rattray was accurately forecasting the future of lifeboats but not on the Great Lakes. For the last 30-plus years saltwater ships have been using a survival capsule type of lifeboat as a way of abandoning ship. Kept ready on set of rails at the stern of a ship, the crew only has to climb, seal it up and internally release the boat to self launch. Lakers still use lifeboats on davits, the best technology of the last century, although self-inflating life rafts are also carried. Getting into either in the midst of a storm is very difficult.

²⁴*Daily Mining Journal* (Marquette), November 24, 1913.
²⁵*Daily Mining Journal* (Marquette), November 15, 1913.
²⁶*Marquette Chronicle*, November 15, 1913; *Daily Mining Journal* (Marquette), November 18, 1913.
²⁷*Marquette Chronicle*, November 15, 1913.
²⁸*Marquette Chronicle*, November 15, 1913.
²⁹*Marquette Chronicle*, December 2, 1913.
³⁰*Marquette Chronicle*, November 9-15, 1913; June 4, 1919; *Evening News* (Sault Ste. Marie, Michigan), June 5, 1919.
³¹*Daily Mining Journal* (Marquette), November 15, 1913.
³²*Daily Mining Journal* (Marquette), November 15, 1913.
³³In the case of a storm-wracked vessel, "migrate" is a polite term for "thunderous rush."
³⁴aka "rolling her guts out."
³⁵*Coast Seamen's Journal; a Journal of Seamen, by Seamen, For Seamen*, Volume 27, 1914.

CHAPTER 9

¹*Buzzfeed*, September 6, 2013.
²*U-656* was the first U-boat sunk by the U.S. Navy after our entry to World War II. Finding it is a long-term goal of the group.
³The 429-foot steamer *Superior City* sank in Whitefish Bay, Lake Superior, on August 20, 1920, after a collision with the steamer *Willis L. King*.
⁴The 420-foot steamer *John B. Cowle* was rammed and sunk a mile northwest of Whitefish Point, Lake Superior, by the steamer *Isaac M. Scott* in fog on July 12, 1909.
⁵The 729-foot *Edmund Fitzgerald* was lost with all 29 hands in a terrific Lake Superior storm on November 10, 1975.
⁶The 420-foot steamer *Cyprus* sank 19 miles off Deer Park, Lake Superior, in a strong gale on October 11, 1907, with the loss of 20 of 21 crew.
⁷*Duluth News Tribune*, June 8, 2013.
⁸The 242-foot *Olive Jeanette* was the tow of steamer *Iosco* when she foundered in a terrific gale on September 2, 1905, with all hands near the Huron Islands, Lake Superior. The *Iosco* was also lost with all hands. The 206-foot *Moonlight* was under tow by the steamer *Volunteer* when she broke her hawser, sinking in a terrific gale. *Volunteer* saved the *Moonlight* crew before she foundered.
⁹The 246-foot wooden steamer *A.A. Parker* sank in a gale off Grand Marais, Michigan, on September 19, 1903. She was located by a search group in 2001, but the location had been kept secret.

Bibliography

American Lloyds, *Record of American and Foreign Ships, 1907*, American Bureau of Shipping, New York.

American Ship Building, Lorain, http://shipbuildinghistory.com/history/shipyards/2large/inactive/amshiplorain.htm.

The American Welding Society, https://www.aws.org/about/blockbuster.html.

Antigo Daily Journal, not dated.

Annual Report U.S. Life-Saving Service, 1914.

Argus file, Stonehouse Collection.

John P. Beck, "They Fought for Their Work, Upper Peninsula Iron Ore Trimmers," *Michigan History Magazine*, January-February 1989, 25-31.

Harvey C. Beeson, *Beeson's Inland Marine Directory, 1913*.

Gershom Bradford, *The Mariner's Dictionary*. Weathervane Books: New York, 1962.

David G. Brown, *White Hurricane: A Great Lakes November Gale and America's Deadliest Maritime Disaster*, International Marine Publishing: New York, 2012, 236.

Buffalo News, October 19, 2013.

Blue Book of American Shipping, Cleveland, 1907.

Bruce W. Bowlus, *Iron Ore Transport on the Great Lakes: The Development of a Delivery System to Feed American Industry*. McFarlane and Company, New York, 2010.

Bulk Carrier Guide, http://www.bulkcarrierguide.com/cargo.html.

Donald L. Canney, *U.S. Coast Guard and Revenue Marine Cutters, 1790-1935*, Annapolis, MD: Naval Institute Press, 1995.

Cargo Handbook, http://www.cargohandbook.com/index.php/Iron_ore_%28fines%29.

Carruthers file, Stonehouse Collection.

Cleveland Plain Dealer, November 6-December 2, 1913

Chesterton Tribune, October 8, 2013.

Coast Seamen's Journal; a Journal of Seamen, by Seamen, for Seamen, Volume 27, 1914.

Cornell Daily Sun, December 6, 1913.

Cyprus, http://www.shipwreckmuseum.com/cyprus.

Cyprus file, Stonehouse Collection.

The *Cyprus* History, http://www.boatnerd.com/pictures/historic/Cyprus/Part13-14.htm.

Daily Mining Gazette (Houghton), November 8-18, 1913.

Daily Mining Journal (Marquette), November 5-December 15, 1913; June 10, July 2, 2013.

Detroit Free Press, November 8-18, 1913.

Daily Observer (Sarnia), November 8-December 10, 1913.

William R. Deedler, "Hell Hath No Fury Like a Great Lakes Fall Storm, Great Lakes White Hurricane: November 1913." National Weather Service Office, undated.

Disston Crucible, a Magazine for Millmen, Vol. 3-4, February 1914.

Timothy R. Dring, "Trial by Fire and Ice: The U.S. Life-Saving Service's Type E Motor Lifeboats and Their Employment in the Great Lakes Storm of 1913, *Wreck and Rescue Journal*, December 2013.

Duluth Herald, November 8-18, 1913.

Duluth News-Tribune, August 16, 1906, June 6, 8, November 8-December 3, 1913.

Jarrod Eliason, interview, November 2013.

Jerry Eliason, interview, November 2013.

Evening News (Sault Ste. Marie, Michigan), June 5, Novmber 22, 1913.

"Efforts to Preserve *J.P. Ford* Ended," AGLMH E-Newsletter August 2014.

William Forsythe, "A Voyage into History with the *Cyprus*," unpublished manuscript, Stonehouse Collection.

"Fresh Fears Over Liquefaction," *The London P&I Club*, January 2014.

The Globe (Toronto), January 1, 1898.

John O. Greenwood, *The Fleet Histories, Volume Six*, Cleveland: Freshwater Press, 1995.

Henry B. Smith file, Stonehouse Collection.

History of Bay County, Michigan, H.R. Page, 1883; *History of Bay County – Bay City Illustrated*, Bay City (Michigan). Board of Trade, C.&J. Gregory Company, n.d.

Huelett Iron Ore Unloaders, https://www.asme.org/getmedia/59a21de6-56b6-4da8-a4d8-520b74c3e86e/199-Hulett-Ore-Unloaders.aspx.

Huronic file, Stonehouse Collection.

Inforum, October 6, 2013.

Iron Ore Trade Review, May 3, 1906.

Debbie Allyn Jett, The Great Lakes Storm of 1913 and the Wreck of the *L.C. Waldo*, *Wreck and Rescue Journal*, December 2013.

Journal of the Society of Naval Engineers, Delivered Paper, "Steamers of the Great Lakes as Regards Strength," Washington, D.C., 1894.

Journal of the U.S. Life-Saving Station at Deer Park, October 8-November 10, 1907.

Journal of the U.S. Life-Saving Service Station at Eagle Harbor, November 9-14, 1913.

Journal of the U.S. Life-Saving Service Station at Grand Marais, November 8-12, 1913.

Journal of the U.S. Life-Saving Service at Marquette, November 8-18, 1913.

Journal of the U.S. Life-Saving Service Station at Portage, November 9-14.

Journal of the U.S. Life-Saving Station at Two-Heart River, October 8-November 10, 1907.

Captain James Kennedy, steamer *Peter White*, letter to Mr. A.F. Harvey, assistant general manager, Pittsburgh Steamship Company, n.d.

Keweenaw County Historical Society, KCHS Papers, n.d.

L.C. Waldo file, Stonehouse Collection.

"The Large Canadian Lake Steamer *James Carruthers*," *Marine Engineering Log*, Volume 19.

John W. Larson, *Essayons, A History of the Detroit District U.S. Army Corps of Engineers*, U.S. Army Corps of Engineers, Detroit District, 1981.

Leafield file, Stonehouse Collection.

Legendary Locals of Bay City, Arcadia Press: Charleston, S.C., n.d.

Liberty Ship Problems, http://en.wikipedia.org/wiki/Liberty_ship#Problems.

Ludington Daily News, April 18, 1906, November 3, 1983.

"Marine Time: Bennetts Remembered as Lake Superior Hero," Antigodailyjournal.com.

Marquette Chronicle, November 8-21, December 2, 1913, June 4, 1919.

McGean file, Stonehouse Collection.

Ken Merryman, interview, November 2013.

The Mining World, May 19, 1906.

Monkshaven file, Stonehouse Collection.

Captain W.T. Mooney, steamer *Andaste*, letter to Mr. A.F. Harvey, assistant general manager, Pittsburgh Steamship Company, n.d.

National Weather Service Office, http://www.crh.noaa.gov/dtx/stm_1913.php.

NOAA Central Library, U.S. Daily Weather Maps Project, http://docs.lib.noaa.gov/rescue/dwm/data_rescue_daily_weather_maps.html.

North Star Port, Summer 2014.

Owen Sound Sun, May 27, 1913.

Pacific Marine Review, Volume 16, 1919.

Perry 200, http://www.perry200.com/.

Kathleen Pletsch, *Centennial Tribute to the Victims of the Storm*, Goderich, Ontario, Great Lakes Storm Remembrance Committee, 2013.

Port Huron Times-Herald, November 7-December 10, 1913.

Perry F. Powers, *History of Northern Michigan and Its People Volume 3*, Chicago, Lewis Publishing Co., 1912.

Price file, Stonehouse Collection.

Regina file, Stonehouse Collection.

C. Fred Rydholm, *Superior Heartland, Volume II*, Marquette, Michigan: privately published by C. Fred Rydholm, 1989.

L.A. Sawyer and W.H. Mitchell, *The Liberty Ships*, Cornell Maritime Press, Cambridge, MD, 1970.

Michael Schumacker, *November's Fury, The Deadly Great Lakes Hurricane of 1913*, Minneapolis: University of Minnesota Press, 2013

Scotch Boiler, http://en.wikipedia.org/wiki/Scotch_marine_boiler.

Paul W. Schopp, email to author, June 8, 1997.

Secretary of the Treasury, letter to Captain Charles A. Tucker, December 5, 1913.

Captain F.B. Selee, steamer *Alexander McDougall*, letter to Mr. A.F. Harvey, assistant general manager, Pittsburgh Steamship Company, n.d.

Spokane file, Stonehouse Collection.

Star Beacon, July 8, 2012.

Steamship *J.B. Ford*, http://www.steamshipjbfordhistoricalsurvey.com/.

"Shipwreck Believed Found in Lake Superior 100 Years Later," Fox News, June 10, 2013.

Storm Meteorology, http://www.regions.noaa.gov/great-lakes/?page_id=1774.

Transactions of the Royal Institution of Naval Architects Volume 39, American Society of Naval Architects and Marine Engineers, 1897.

Turret Chief file, Stonehouse Collection.

U.S. Coast Guard, Storm Flags, http://www.uscg.mil/news/stormcenter/.

U.S. Department of Agriculture, Weather Bureau, Daily Local Record, Marquette, Michigan, November 6-13, 1913.

U.S. Navy Fact File P-3 Orion, http://www.navy.mil/navydata/fact_display.asp?cid=1100&tid=1400&ct=1.

Welcome to the USS *Defender*, http://www.defender.navy.mil/default.aspx.

Captain F.A. West, steamer *William G. Mather*, letter to Mr. A.F. Harvey, assistant general manager, Pittsburgh Steamship Company, n.d.

Wexford, http://www.shipwreckwexford.ca/.

Wexford file, Stonehouse Collection.

The "White Hurricane" Storm of November 1913, A Numerical Model Retrospective, Richard Wagenmaker, NWS Detroit; Dr. Greg Mann, NWS Detroit, http://www.crh.noaa.gov/images/dtx/climate/1913Retrospective.pdf.

William D. Wilkerson and Timothy R. Dring, Commander USN, Retired, *American Coastal Rescue Craft*, (University Press of Florida: Gainesville, 2013).

William Nottingham file, Stonehouse Collection.

David H. Wollman and Donald R. Inman, *Portraits in Steel: an Illustrated History of the Jones & Laughlin Steel Company*, Kent, Ohio: Kent State University Press, 1999.

Wreck Report – Steamer *Cyprus*, U.S. Life-Saving Station Deer Park, October 11, 1907.

Wreck Report – Steamer *Henry B. Smith*, U.S. Life-Saving Service.

Richard J. Wright, *Freshwater Whales, A History of the American Ship Building Company and Its Predecessors*. Kent State University Press, 1969.

1913 Storm file, Stonehouse Collection.

1913 Lake Carriers Annual Report, 1914.

Index

All boats listed under Vessels

A
Acme Transit Company 25, 161
Aerial Lift Bridge 27
William H. Alexander 130
John C. Alfsen 123
Alpena, Michigan 65, 70, 130
A. McMillen & Sons 63
American Ship Building Company 17, 20-21, 24-25, 56, 62, 65, 123, 141, 143, 147-148, 166, 175
American Steel Barge Company 148, 150
Angus Island 74-75
Apostle Islands 185, 195, 196
Ashburton Bay 194
Ashland, Wisconsin 83-84
Ashtabula, Ohio 13-14, 103
Au Sable Point 107

B
B-52 Stratofortress 4
Brendon Baillod 186
Captain Baird 75
Charles Baker 74
C.C. Balfour 25
Battle Island 84
Bay City, Michigan 18, 23-24, 26, 88
Bay Ship Building Company 53
Beausoleil Island 75
Beaver Lake 125
John Beck 122
Randy Beebe 2, 4
Beeson's Marine Directory 26, 176
Alex Begg 28
Thomas W. Bennetts 100, 110, 122
Bete Grise 97, 113, 124
Big Bay, Michigan 96, 187

Big Point 85
Sadie Black 66, 68
W.A. Black 62
Brockville, Ontario 26-27
Harry Brousseau 148
Alexander E. Brown 13
C.D. Brown 155, 161-162, 165-166, 176
Brown Fast Plant 13
Buffalo, New York 16, 18, 43, 45-47, 76
Buffalo Union Dry Dock Company 16, 18, 76
John Burke 127
Charles W. Butler 46

C
Morris Call 128
Calumet, Michigan 101
Bruce Cameron 58-61
Canada Steamship Lines 79, 192
Cape Croker 61
Cape Race, Newfoundland 187
George Carey iii
Caribou Island 78, 80
Caribou Shoal 167
E.D. Carter 166
Charles Cattanach iii, 107
Chadburn 32
Champion Hoist 13
Chicago, Illinois 14, 18, 49-50, 54, 73, 74
Chicago Ship Building Company 18
Chocolay River 125
Henry Cleary 106-107, 124-126, 128
Cleveland, Ohio 9-10, 13-14, 16-18, 20, 28, 62, 83, 88-89, 102, 127, 130, 143, 162-163, 176, 193
Collingwood, Ontario 57, 74
Conneaut, Ohio 15

Copper Harbor, Michigan 119, 121
Corsica Shoal 73
Corunna, Ontario 107
Peter Costandakis iii
John Cousins iii
A. Craigee 81
Captain Crawford 72-73
Crisp's Point 79
T.J. Cullen 81
Mary Ella Cutting 28

D
Daily Mining Journal 163-164, 167
Deckerville, Minnesota 107
Thomas Deegan 67
Deer Park, Michigan 77, 139
Delaware, Michigan 97
DeTour, Michigan 54, 58, 130
Detroit, Michigan 18, 29, 133, 166
Detroit Ship Building Company 18
Donelan Wave Model 41
Door Peninsula 50
Doxford & Sons 57
John W. Duddleson 89-91, 94
Duluth, Minnesota ii, 12, 27, 62, 82, 91-92, 148, 156, 159, 178, 195
Duluth, South Shore and Atlantic Railroad 12, 91

E
Eagle Harbor, Michigan iii, 97-98, 100, 110-111, 116, 118-123
Eagle Mine 8
Eagle River, Michigan 193
Jarrod Eliason 185, 190
Jerry Eliason iii, 184-196
Karen Eliason 187-188

209

Erie, Pennsylvania 48
Escanaba, Michigan 50, 128

F
Fairport, Ohio 13
F.B. Spear Dock 103
Bernard Foley 89
Fort Gratiot, Michigan 62, 69, 72, 164
Fort William, Ontario 58, 65, 70, 74-75, 192
Dan Fountain 4, 191
Charles Fox 103-105, 109
John Frahm 67
Martin Freeman iii
F.W. Wheeler Company 88

G
John Gallagher iii, 126, 128
Georgian Bay 53-54, 57, 61, 70, 74-75, 123, 164, 196
W.R. Gilcher 139
Gilchrist Transportation Company 196
G.J. Grammer 134
Anthony F. Glaza 110, 118, 122
Glenview Naval Air Station 3
Globe Iron Works 16, 18, 193
Goderich, Ontario 55-56, 58-61, 72, 136-137
William Gordon 130, 132
Goulais Point 126, 168
Grand Bend, Ontario 59-60
Grand Island 126, 156
Grand Marais, Michigan 121, 126-127
Grand Truck Railway 26
Granite Island 167-168
Ulysses S. Grant 36
Great Lakes Environmental Research Laboratory 41
Great Lakes Shipwreck Historical Society 149-150, 178
Great Lakes Shipwreck Preservation Society 186
Paul Guetch 52
Gull Rock 90-93, 95, 97, 111-112, 119, 124, 178

H
William Hagan 65
Alexander Hamilton 134
Hamilton, Ontario 55, 105
Hancock, Michigan 68, 119
Harbor Beach, Michigan 42, 64, 67-68
Harry H. Haskin iii, 105, 126
Hawgoods 20, 24-25, 28, 161-164
Hines Lumber Company 81
George Holpainen 122
Hoover and Mason Company 14
Carl Hoppel iii
Houghton, Michigan 113
George H. Hulett 14
Hulett 14-15
Huron Cement Company 28
Huron City 67
Huron Islands 81, 165

I
Ile Parisienne 75
Institute of Naval Architecture 144
Inverhuron, Ontario 54
Isle Royale, Michigan 46, 74, 79, 84, 126, 154, 185-186, 193

J
William Jensen 46
Dan Johnson 125, 165-166
P.E. Johnson 113
Warren C. Jones 80
Rufus Judson iii, 105
Otto Julius iii
Sebastian Junger 34

K
Edward Kanaby 69
KC-135 Stratotanker 4
Charles Keefer 89
Chris Keenan 49
Roy Kelly iii
James Kennedy 156
Keweenaw Peninsula 89-91, 95, 97-98, 105, 108-111, 113-114, 116, 118-120, 124, 158, 168-170, 178-181

Keweenaw Point 89-90, 95, 105, 110, 116, 119, 168, 178
Keystone Bay 119
Joseph Kidd 149-151
Kincardine, Ontario 52, 54
Kingston, Ontario 70
Knife Island 193
Charles Kumpula 123

L
Lackawanna Steamship Company 147
Lac La Belle 97
Lake Carriers' Association 20, 35, 127, 129, 134-135
Lake Erie 36, 41-44, 46, 48, 134-135
Lake Huron 27, 36, 41-43, 52-54, 56-58, 60, 62-63, 69-72, 103, 128, 130, 134, 137, 140, 142, 157, 173, 181
Lake Huron Hotel 69
Lake Michigan 41, 49, 139-141
Lake Superior ii, iv, vii, 1, 3, 5, 8, 10, 12, 17, 25, 29, 41-43, 52, 54, 56-58, 63, 65, 68, 70, 74, 79, 82, 88, 102, 105, 107, 114, 121, 128, 139, 142, 145-146, 152, 166, 170, 185, 187, 194
Lake Superior and Ishpeming Railroad 12
Andrew Leahy 46
Cornelius Leahy 46
Albert Lembke 94
Chris Leofen iii
Lexington, Michigan 53, 64
Paul Liedtke 123
Lime Island 54, 58
Lloyd's of London 144
Lorain, Ohio 13-14, 16-17, 19-21, 24, 53, 56, 62, 65, 123, 134, 141, 143, 147, 166, 175
James Lowe 53
Ludington, Michigan 24

Ludington Woodenware
Company 24
Denny Lynn 63
S.A. Lyons 54

M
Peter Mackey 46
Mrs. Mackie 92
Mamaimse Point 166
Manitou Islands 139
Matt Maralick iii
The Marine Review 176
Marquette Chronicle 96, 162-164
Marquette Iron Range 8-10, 146
Marquette, Michigan iv, 2, 4, 8-12, 18, 29-31, 43, 48, 57, 86, 89, 91, 93, 96, 102-106, 108, 113, 119, 121, 124-128, 145-146, 156, 161-165, 167-168, 177-181, 195
Oscar Marshall 123
Marvin Island 193
A.C. May 69-70
Gibbs McAdoo 122
A. McArthur 65
E.H. McConkey 63
Thomas H. McCormick 111, 113, 123
John McDonald 123
William McDonald 72
James McGee iii
Meaford, Ontario 61
Mendota, Michigan 97
Menominee, Michigan 49
Ken Merryman iii, 98, 184-186, 193
Mesabi Iron Range 145-146
Michigan Island 84, 195
Michigan Pipe Company 23
Michipicoten Island 84, 114, 124
Midland, Ontario 53-54, 70
Milwaukee, Wisconsin 65
Minnesota Point 195
Montreal, Quebec 192
W.T. Mooney 130, 133
A.C. Mosher 95-97, 111, 119
Mathew Mulholland 149

Munising, Michigan 43, 125, 166
Muskegon, Michigan 44

N
National Bicycle Company 23
National Geospatial Intelligence Agency 187
National Oceanic and Atmospheric Administration iv, vii, 35-36, 38, 40-43, 98, 102-104, 110-111, 114, 116
Bert Nelson 112
Chauncey R. Ney 56
Niagara River 48
Charles J. Nilsen iii
Captain Noble 76-79
Northern Navigation Company 79-80

O
J.R. Oldham 139, 143-145, 151, 156-157, 169, 171-172, 174
Andrew Olsen iii
John H. Olsen iii
Otter Head 82, 84
James Owen iii, 5, 25-30, 32, 57, 80, 89, 91, 93, 101-102, 105-109, 113, 115, 119, 127-128, 154-155, 160-163, 165, 168, 172, 176-178, 180-181
Mrs. James Owen 128

P
P-2 Neptune 3
P-3 Orion 2-3
P-3A Orion 3
P-3B Orion 3
P-8A Poseidon 4
Henry Padberg 123
Thomas Paddington 120
Pentwater, Michigan 24, 49
Pequaming, Michigan 112
Lawrence Perry iii
John Persons 70
Pictured Rocks National Lakeshore 43, 125, 142
Pie Island 76

Pittsburgh Steamship Company 82
Charles Pitz 145-147
Plum Island, Wisconsin 50
Point Abbaye 81
Pointe aux Barques 42-43, 65, 68, 142
Point Iroquois 79-80
Portage Lake 81, 111
Port Arthur, Ontario 58, 74
Port Austin, Michigan 66-67
Port Clark, Ontario 58
Port Franks, Ontario 64, 71, 73
Port Huron, Michigan 36, 64, 72-73, 152
Port Sanilac, Michigan 64
Powell's Point 125
William Powell 125
Presque Isle 12, 86, 104, 124-125

R
Racine-Truscott-Shell Lake Boat Company 44
Charles E. Rayburn iii, 108
W.E. Redway 143-144, 169, 174
Mrs. Arthur Rice 92
Roby Transportation Company 88
Rock of Ages 46, 84
Royal National Lifeboat Institute 100
Rydholm Brothers 101
Carl Rydholm 101

S
Saginaw, Michigan 24
St. Clair River 60, 63, 73
St. Lawrence River 26
St. Martin Island 49
St. Marys River 9, 26, 58, 124, 177
Sandusky, Ohio 56, 126
Sarnia, Ontario 58, 63-64
Sault Ste. Marie, Michigan 74, 83, 89, 127, 130, 178
Sawtooth Reef 193-194
F.D. Selee 82

Edward Shipley iii, 107
John Shirl iii
Shot Point 86, 125
David M. Small 123
Henry Bentley Smith 24
Henry Bloomfield Smith 23
Hezekiah B. Smith 25
H.B. Smith Company 25
Kraig Smith iii, 184, 186
Milton Smith 62
Smith Steamship
    Company 24-25
Fred C. Sollman 123
Sombra, Ontario 107
South Manitou Island 50
South Sandy Island 75
Robert Louis Stevenson 99
Albert Stiglin 152, 154, 178
John A. Stuffelbeam 50
Sulphur Island 70
Sunderland, England 57
Superior Ship Building
    Company 17
Superior, Wisconsin 18, 82-83, 145, 150

T

John Tait iii
Tawas, Michigan 56
Thedford, Ontario 65
John Thompson 55-56
Thomas Thompson 55
Three Sisters 42
Thunder Bay, Lake
    Huron 70
Thunder Bay, Ontario 53-54, 57-58, 65, 74, 142, 196
Thunder Cape 193
Toledo, Ohio 14, 16, 18, 68, 154
Toledo Ship Building
    Company 18
Toronto, Ontario 43, 55, 57, 144
David Trotter 56
Trowbridge Island 75, 193
Charles A. Tucker 98, 100-101, 107, 110-111, 116, 122-123

Two Harbors,
    Minnesota 88, 90, 195
Two-Hearted River 79

U

U.S. Army Signal Corps 38
U.S. Department of
    Commerce 39
U.S. Life-Saving Service vii
U.S. Navy vi, 2-3
U.S. Revenue Marine
    Service 134
U.S. Steamboat Inspection
    Service 178
U.S. Weather Bureau 35-36, 102, 129-132, 136

V

Vermilion, Ohio 152
Vessels
    A.A. Parker 192
    A.H. Febert 156
    A.H. Hawgood 25
    Alberta 74
    Alexander McDougall 82-83
    Algoma 74, 193
    A.M. Byers 81
    Andaste 130, 133
    Andrea Gail 34
    Arcadian 70
    Argus 42, 52-53, 142
    Asian Forest 174
    Augustus B. Wolvin 17
    Benjamin Noble 189, 195
    Black Rose 174
    G.J. Boyce 49-50
    Burlington 196
    Butterfield 196
    Carl D. Bradley 136, 140-141, 158, 170, 173
    Champion 112, 116, 118-119, 121
    Champlain 47
    Charles L. Hutchinson 143
    Charles S. Price 42, 55-56, 62-65, 69-70, 134, 143, 173
    Choctaw 103-105, 109, 145, 177, 179
    *Col. James M.
        Schoonmaker* 154

Cornell 76-79
Cyprus vii, 142, 145-147, 149-150, 155, 175-179, 188, 192
Daniel Hebard 112-113, 119
Daniel J. Morrell 136, 140-142, 158, 170, 173
David Boyd 178
Defender 4, 5
Denmark 105, 145, 177, 179-180
D.O. Mills 42, 69
D.R. Hanna 142
Edmund Fitzgerald 3, 42, 128-129, 136, 138, 144, 158-159, 167, 178, 182
Edward Y. Townsend 140-142
Edwin F. Holmes 20, 27, 29, 155, 160-163, 165, 176
Elise 57
Favorite 68
Fayette Brown 143
Frank H. Goodyear 142
Fred G. Hartwell 79
Frontenac 125
George Stephenson 95, 97, 111, 124, 145, 178
George Tulane 122
H.A. Hawgood 25
Halstead 50-51
Hamonic 75
Harvester 114
Harvey D. Goulder 21
Henry A. Hawgood 20, 64, 69, 164
Henry B. Smith iii-vii, 1-2, 4-6, 8, 20-21, 23-31, 33, 53, 57, 69, 80, 86, 89, 91-94, 96, 101-102, 104-109, 113-114, 116, 119, 124-129, 138, 140-143, 145, 147, 149-158, 160, 162-178, 180-182, 184-189, 191-192, 196

Henry Steinbrenner 152-154, 158, 175-179
Heyboy 185
Howard M. Hanna Jr. 42, 65-67
H.P. Hope 158
Huronic 79-80
Hydrus 42, 53, 142
Illinois 3, 50
Iosco 165-166
Isaac M. Scott 42, 65, 142, 157
James B. Wood 142
James Carruthers vi, 43, 53-56
James H. Martin 49
Jane Miller 60-61
J.H. Sheulle 54
J.J. Jones 61-62
J.M. Jenks 70, 152, 164-165
John A. McGean 42, 56, 142
John B. Cowle 188
John B. Ford 20, 28, 161-162
Joseph Sellwood 21-22
J.T. Hutchinson 79
Judge Hart 189, 194-195
J.W. Westcott 29
Kaministiquia 58
Kamloops 186, 192
Kenosha 49
L.C. Waldo vii, 88-96, 98, 101, 105-106, 111, 116-120, 123-126, 166, 174, 178
Leafield 62, 74-76, 125
Lewis Woodruff 142
Lightship No. 82 43-48
Loftus Cuddy 21-22
Louisiana 50
Loyal 121
M.A. Hanna 85
Major 81
Maple 55
Margaret 122
Mataafa 92
Matoa 43, 68
Matthew Andrews 73
Maumee 155
Michigan 134

Mohawk Deer (L.C. Waldo) 123
Monkshaven 75-76
Moonlight 192, 195
Morrill 134-135
Nantucket 44
Niagara 48, 134
Niña 48
Northern Queen 70, 72-73
Nottingham 75-76
Olive Jeanette 165, 192
Olympic 44
Onoko 15-16, 193-194
Ontario 196
Peter A.B. Widener 85
Peter White 156
Pinta 48
Plymouth 48-49
Princeton 85
Quincy A. Shaw 142
Ralph S. Caulkins 165
Regina 42, 55-57, 62-64, 69-70
R.E. Schuck 142
Riverton (L.C. Waldo) 123
R.J. Hackett 10, 15
Rosecrans 122
Santa Maria 48
Saxona 126-127
Scotiadoc 196
Simon Langell 82
Sir Trevor Dawson 193
Spokane 16
Success 98, 110, 112, 116-118, 121
Superior City 159, 188
Susquehanna 16
Sylvania 43, 80-81
Tempest 121
T.H. Camp 186
Theano 75, 193
Thomas Friant 195
Titanic 44, 139
Turret Chief 118-120
Tuscarora 126
U-656 187
Volunteer 195
W.A. Hawgood 25
Western Reserve 139
Wexford 43, 57-59, 62
William A. Hawgood 20

William C. Moreland 193
William Edenborn 81
William G. Mather 83-84
William Nottingham 75
Willis B. Boyer 154
Winona 86
W.R. Woodford 25

W
Washington Harbor 50
Weather Research and Forecast Modeling System 40
West Bay City, Michigan 81, 141
West Bay Ship Building Company 18
Western Steamship Company 57
Westerville, Ontario 49
F.A. West 83-85
Collin S. Westrope 123
F. Wheeler 81
Whirleys 13
Whitefish Bay, Michigan 27, 75, 79, 81
Whitefish Point 43, 74, 76-77, 79, 80-83, 85, 103, 107, 126, 166
Wiarton, Ontario 61
Hugh M. Williams 46, 48
George Wilmott 58
Grace Wilmott 58
Woodrow Wilson 132-134
William H. Wright 53-54
Wyandotte, Michigan 18

Y
H.J. Yaques 79

Z
Joseph Zink iii, 107, 109

About the Author

Frederick Stonehouse holds a Master of Arts degree in History from Northern Michigan University and has authored numerous books on American maritime history. Among them are *Wreck Ashore, the U.S. Life-Saving Service on the Great Lakes* and *Shipwreck of the* Mesquite, *Death of a Coast Guard Cutter*, published by Lake Superior Port Cities Inc., as well as the *Wreck of the* Edmund Fitzgerald.

He has also been a consultant for both the U.S. National Park Service and Parks Canada and an "on air" expert for The History Channel and other broadcast outlets. His articles have been published in *Lake Superior Magazine* and *Wreck and Rescue Journal*. He is a member of the Board of Directors of the Marquette Maritime Museum and the U.S. Life-Saving Service Heritage Association.

He has been honored with the Association for Great Lakes Maritime History award for historic interpretation in recognition of his many contributions to the field and as the Marine Historian of the Year by the Detroit Marine Historical Society. Most recently he was presented the 2014 "Distinguished Alumni Award" by Northern Michigan University.

Fred teaches Great Lakes maritime history at Northern Michigan University and is an active consultant for numerous Great Lakes-oriented projects and programs.

He resides in Marquette with his wife, Lois.

From Lake Superior Port Cities Inc.
Since 1979

Lake Superior Magazine
A bimonthly, regional publication covering the shores along Michigan, Minnesota, Wisconsin and Ontario

Lake Superior Travel Guide
An annually updated mile-by-mile guide

Lake Superior, The Ultimate Guide to the Region, Third Edition
Softcover: ISBN 978-1-938229-17-6

Hugh E. Bishop:
The Night the Fitz Went Down
Softcover: ISBN 978-0-942235-37-1

By Water and Rail:
A History of Lake County, Minnesota
Hardcover: ISBN 978-0-942235-48-7
Softcover: ISBN 978-0-942235-42-5

Haunted Lake Superior
Softcover: ISBN 978-0-942235-55-5

Haunted Minnesota
Softcover: ISBN 978-0-942235-71-5

Beryl Singleton Bissell:
A View of the Lake
Softcover: ISBN 978-0-942235-74-6

Bonnie Dahl:
Bonnie Dahl's Superior Way, Fourth Edition:
A Crusing Guide to Lake Superior
Softcover: ISBN 978-0-942235-92-0

Joy Morgan Dey, Nikki Johnson:
Agate: What Good Is a Moose?
Hardcover: ISBN 978-0-942235-73-9

Daniel R. Fountain:
Michigan Gold & Silver,
Mining in the Upper Peninsula
Softcover: ISBN 978-1-938229-16-9

Chuck Frederick:
Spirit of the Lights
Softcover: ISBN 978-0-942235-11-1

Marvin G. Lamppa:
Minnesota's Iron Country
Softcover: ISBN 978-0-942235-56-2

Daniel Lenihan:
Shipwrecks of Isle Royale National Park
Softcover: ISBN 978-0-942235-18-0

Betty Lessard:
Betty's Pies Favorite Recipes, Second Edition
Softcover: ISBN 978-1-938229-18-3

Mike Link & Kate Crowley:
Going Full Circle:
A 1,555-mile Walk Around the World's Largest Lake
Softcover: ISBN 978-0-942235-23-4

James R. Marshall:
Shipwrecks of Lake Superior, Second Edition
Softcover: ISBN 978-0-942235-67-8

Lake Superior Journal: Views from the Bridge
Softcover: ISBN 978-0-942235-40-1

Mark Phillips:
The Old Rittenhouse Inn Cookbook:
Meals & Memories from the Historic Bayfield B&B
Softcover: ISBN 978-1-938229-19-0

Kathy Rice:
The Pie Place Café Cookbook:
Food & Stories Seasoned by the North Shore
Softcover: ISBN 978-1-938229-04-6

Howard Sivertson:
Driftwood: Stories Picked Up Along the Shore
Hardcover: ISBN 978-0-942235-91-3

Schooners, Skiffs & Steamships:
Stories along Lake Superior's Water Trails
Hardcover: ISBN 978-0-942235-51-7

Tales of the Old North Shore
Hardcover: ISBN 978-0-942235-29-6

The Illustrated Voyageur
Hardcover: ISBN 978-0-942235-43-2

Once Upon an Isle:
The Story of Fishing Families on Isle Royale
Hardcover: ISBN 978-0-962436-93-2

Frederick Stonehouse:
The Last Laker: Finding the Deadliest Storm's Lost Shipwreck
Softcover: ISBN 978-1-938229-23-7

Wreck Ashore: United States
Life-Saving Service,
Legendary Heroes of the Great Lakes
Softcover: ISBN 978-0-942235-58-6

Shipwreck of the Mesquite
Softcover: ISBN 978-0-942235-10-4

Haunted Lakes (the original)
Softcover: ISBN 978-0-942235-30-2

Haunted Lakes II
Softcover: ISBN 978-0-942235-39-5

Haunted Lake Michigan
Softcover: ISBN 978-0-942235-72-2

Haunted Lake Huron
Softcover: ISBN 978-0-942235-79-1

Julius F. Wolff Jr.:
Julius F. Wolff Jr.'s Lake Superior Shipwrecks
Hardcover: ISBN 978-0-942235-02-9
Softcover: ISBN 978-0-942235-01-2

www.LakeSuperior.com
1-888-BIG LAKE (888-244-5253)
Outlet Store: 310 E. Superior St., Duluth, MN 55802